The Philadelphia Inquirer

JALEN HURTS
Rare Bird

Heather Khalifa / Staff Photographer

Jalen Hurts acknowledges the home crowd after the Eagles posted a 38-7 playoff rout of the Giants on Jan. 21, 2023. Three seasons after he became a surprising second-round draft pick, Hurts was playing in the Super Bowl. (David Maialetti / Staff Photographer)

The Philadelphia Inquirer

Lisa Hughes, Publisher & CEO

Gabriel Escobar, Editor, Senior vice president

Charlotte Sutton, Managing editor

Patrick Kerkstra, Managing editor

Mike Huang, Managing editor/Sports

Gary Potosky, Assistant managing editor/Sports

John Roberts and Jim Swan, book editors

Diamond Leung, Eagles editor

Gustav Elvin, DeAntae Prince, Kerith Gabriel, Maria McIlwain, contributing editors

Suzette Moyer, Design director

Danese Kenon, Managing editor/Visuals

Frank Wiese, Deputy director of video and photography

Writers: Josh Tolentino, EJ Smith, Jeff McLane, Marcus Hayes, Matt Breen, Mike Sielski, Ximena Conde

Inquirer staff photographers: Yong Kim, David Maialetti, Monica Herndon, Heather Khalifa, Tyger Williams, Alejandro Alvarez

Contributing photographers: Elizabeth Conley and Jonathan Wilson

This book is available in quantity at special discounts for your group or organization.

For further information, contact:

Triumph Books LLC
814 North Franklin Street
Chicago, Illinois 60610
Phone: (312) 337-0747
www.triumphbooks.com

Printed in U.S.A.
ISBN: 978-1-63727-372-2

Content packaged by Mojo Media, Inc.
Joe Funk: Editor
Jason Hinman: Creative Director

Front cover photo by Steven M. Falk
Back cover photo by David Maialetti

Contents

Introduction

By Jeff McLane

Jalen Hurts had few options as he trotted to his left, two yards from the end zone and from knotting up Super Bowl LVII. There would be little mystery. The Eagles would once again call their quarterback's number and the Chiefs were prepared.

Football played at its highest level has become team sports' version of advanced mathematics. Its biggest game involved countless hours of preparation from players to coaches to analysts of inflated organizations searching for any inch that can provide an edge. The Chiefs-Eagles Super Bowl featured an X's-and-O's sage in Andy Reid on one side and an up-and-coming strategist in Nick Sirianni on the other.

But when the latter needed the most important 72 inches of the season, he followed an elemental rule of coaching: Get the ball into your best player's hands. And the Eagles coach did so without much fuss — much as he did on the preceding touchdown — dialing up Hurts power left. Two Chiefs broke through untouched. The first bounced off Hurts and the still-tender left shoulder that nearly derailed the Eagles just weeks earlier. The second wrapped him up from the side. But the 24-year-old who had endured enough adversity in his brief career to last a lifetime would not go down.

If failure is defined as an absence or lack of success, then what occurred following the Eagles' two-point conversion can be labeled as such. Patrick Mahomes marched the other direction for a go-ahead field goal and Hurts' last-gasp heave hit the ground, setting off a red and gold coronation.

Hurts, though not the victor, was successful in overcoming a costly first-half fumble to deliver his finest performance, and afterward in gracefully accepting defeat. Two months later, the Eagles awarded him with what was then the largest annual contract in NFL history: a five-year extension worth $255 million with $110 million fully guaranteed.

"Money is nice," Hurts said. "Championships are better."

Few saw this future for the Houston native, not when he carried Channelview High to its first playoff appearance in years, or when he won the starting job at Alabama as a freshman, or when he finished runner-up for the Heisman Trophy, or when he supplanted Carson Wentz, or when he guided the Eagles to the postseason in his first full year as QB1, or even during his MVP-caliber third season.

But for those who did, who observed how he played behind an undersized offensive line in high school, or how he handled a benching in the national championship and the loss of his starting job in college, or the scrutiny that comes with being drafted by a franchise that supposedly already had its quarterback, or the innumerable slights that come with playing the toughest position in some of the most passionate football towns in America, it was merely inevitable.

Hurts, most of all, had to believe.

Jalen Hurts tied up Super Bowl LVII with a bruising two-point conversion run with 5 minutes, 15 seconds left. But the Chiefs' own transcendent quarterback, Patrick Mahomes, produced the game-winning drive. (Monica Herndon / Staff Photographer)

"I had a purpose," he said on the eve of the Super Bowl, "before everybody had an opinion."

Over the last three years, from the Eagles' shocking selection of Hurts in the second round of the 2020 draft, to their decidedly less surprising decision to ink him to a franchise-altering second deal, The Inquirer has chronicled his rise in the NFL.

But there have also been stories about his formative years in East Texas, his highs and lows in Tuscaloosa, and his transformation in Norman; anecdotes about his stoicism, his unnerving of Wentz, and his work ethic; and Hurtisms like "Just trying to be a coffee bean," "Keep the main thing the main thing," and lastly, after the Super Bowl loss, "You either win or you learn."

You can find a proverb for almost any failure, but Hurts' journey can't be summed up with an adage even here on these pages. There remain legitimate questions about the young quarterback and the seasons to come. Super Bowls are difficult to reach and one man — no matter how integral — can't engineer that ride alone. But the Eagles have placed their trust in Hurts just as Sirianni did on that fateful two-point try. Their optimism is matched only by this book's publication and subsequent purchase.

We hope you enjoy its contents. ∎

A Tarmac, Xbox, and the LeBron Special

How Oklahoma helped Jalen Hurts become the Eagles' star QB

January 17, 2023 | By Matt Breen

The buses were rumbling, waiting to take the Oklahoma football players — dejected after a stunning loss to an unranked team spoiled their undefeated season — back to campus. They flew home from Kansas State in silence, drudged down the steps to the tarmac, and headed for their rides.

It was a painful day — "Around here, you lose one game and you think someone died," wide receiver Nick Basquine said — and it would be over with a 30-minute bus trip from Oklahoma City to Norman. But before the players reached the buses, the Sooners were stopped on the tarmac by Jalen Hurts.

The quarterback, eye black still smeared on his face, was one of the first players off the chartered flight. He walked to his right, away from the noise of the airplane engines, and told his teammates to follow him.

The players felt as if their 2019 season, which they dreamed would end in the College Football Playoff, was finished. And Hurts had something to say.

"So what?" he said. "Now what?"

Hurts arrived on campus 10 months earlier as a transfer from Alabama, where he lost his starting job on national TV and spent a season as a backup.

Adversity? For Hurts, a seven-point loss in October at Kansas State was hardly that.

The loss, Hurts told the players who surrounded him, happened. They couldn't change the result, but they could control their future. Their attitude, Hurts said, was wrong as they simply expected to win because they thought they were the better team. You can't do that.

The quarterback spoke with conviction on the tarmac without raising his voice. The Sooners had four games remaining, enough time, Hurts said, for the players to adjust their mindsets.

So what? Now what?

"I was ready to fight for him," running back Trey Sermon said.

Cut from a different cloth

Hurts had been on campus for just a few days when he gathered the team after an offseason January practice. Four years later, he enters this Saturday's divisional-round playoff game as one of the NFL's promising young quarterbacks for the top-seeded Eagles.

But then, Hurts was a transfer who had been discarded at his previous stop. He joined Oklahoma

No stranger to pressure, Jalen Hurts became the first freshman quarterback to start under Nick Saban at the University of Alabama. (AP Images)

for his final college season a week after throwing two passes as a backup in Alabama's national championship game loss. A season earlier, he had led the Crimson Tide to the final game but was benched at halftime.

For anyone else, the 12 months that preceded Hurts' arrival to Oklahoma would have been crushing.

"But he's just cut from a little different cloth from most people," said Lincoln Riley, then Oklahoma's head coach. "His attitude, his outlook on things. He has some real perspective for being as young as he is and being thrown into some of the situations that he's been thrown into really early on in life."

The Oklahoma staff watched from afar as Hurts seemed to handle his benching with poise. He said all the right things, didn't question the decision, and waited until after the season to announce his decision to transfer. Hurts seemed to have everything needed to lead a team. And it didn't take long — just one practice — for the coaches to see him fulfill those expectations.

"He got into the huddle, broke the team down," said Shane Beamer, then Riley's assistant head coach for offense. "It was pretty evident then that this guy was about the right stuff. There was no part of me that thought, 'This is a different guy from who we thought we were getting.' He was actually even better."

Building his teammates up

Hurts and Basquine sat together in the grass later that spring, taking off their cleats after the new quarterback threw a series of passes to his new weapon.

Basquine grew up in Norman, walked on to the Sooners, and earned a scholarship before being slowed by injuries. He played with Kyler Murray and Baker Mayfield, two transfer quarterbacks who won the Heisman Trophy at Oklahoma. And now he was catching passes from the QB they thought could be the next one.

"He's like, 'You're one of the best dudes I've ever played with,'" Basquine said. "I'm thinking, 'Well, I know where you just came from and the dudes you've thrown the football to. So you're either lying to me to get me to feel better or you think I'm a pretty good football player.' I chose to take the latter."

Hurts cemented himself in Philadelphia as a leader, bringing a presence to the team almost as soon as he arrived. And that's how he was in Oklahoma, arriving with just a season of eligibility remaining.

He easily could have been a mercenary as he built his stock for the NFL draft. But Hurts, from his first practice to his first throws with a new receiver, invested in his team.

"He helped others believe in themselves even if they didn't believe in themselves. He speaks life into his teammates," Basquine said. "I think that's the biggest thing in this game, especially when you get to D-1 and the NFL. Everyone is good, so it's more the mental side and I think he understands that by speaking life into his teammates, lifting them up."

Not yet the starter

Hurts was a leader, but he wasn't a starter when training camp began. He was the SEC's offensive player of the year as a freshman in 2016 and took two Alabama teams to the College Football Playoff. But Riley told Hurts he would still have to win the job at Oklahoma.

"My mindset was if he's good enough to come be our guy and be what we think he can be, then he would win the job," said Riley, now the head coach at Southern California. "If he's not, then he won't."

Guaranteeing Hurts a job, Riley said, would

Jalen Hurts answers questions during media day for the NCAA College Football Playoff championship game in January 2019. Having been relegated to a backup role at Alabama, Hurts made the decision to transfer to Oklahoma. (AP Images)

have sent a poor message to the rest of the team as they all needed to win their spots. The other QBs, who were on campus before Hurts arrived, would get their shot.

"I actually think he might not have come if we just told him, 'Oh yeah, the job is yours.' Honestly," Riley said. "He would've seen the phony in that and he's super conscious of the locker room, the team, the vibe of the team, the work ethic of the team, the mindset. He would've wanted to earn it even if I said, 'No, it's yours.' That's the attitude."

Hurts won the job three weeks before the start of the season as he answered the coach's challenge to change the way he played. Riley's "Air Raid" offense requires the quarterback to play loose and embrace creativity in the pocket.

Riley spoke to Hurts and his father before he joined the Sooners, telling them how this offense was different from the one he ran at Alabama.

"The best way to explain it is that he's a very intense, process-driven, hyper-focused guy, which obviously has some huge benefits," Riley said. "But at times, I thought it restricted him with the way he played and at times, being a little too robotic.

"There's a system and a method to our offense, but there's a little free-flowing attitude that can help a quarterback as well. It struck me very early on that this kid needs to not change who you are but to have the ability to play free-flowing at times and approach it that way and have fun with it and enjoy it in addition to being focused and playing well."

Hurts bought in, loosened up in the pocket, and finished eighth in the nation in passing yards while leading all quarterbacks in rushing yards. His arm seemed limited at Alabama, which is why he was lifted at halftime of the national championship game when the Crimson Tide were playing from behind.

But the first glimpse of the player he blossomed into with the Eagles — a quarterback who can challenge opponents both on the ground and through the air — came after he became less robotic with Riley.

"If he got anything from us in that year, learning to see the game and approach it a little bit differently, learning to play a little more free-flowing and trusting that, I thought it helped him a lot in his year with us," Riley said. "And I think as I've seen him grow in the NFL, I think that was an important step for him that he did a great job with us."

Soul food and Xbox

Hurts was no longer robotic on the field, but he still seemed a bit automated away from it. His postgame news conferences — similar to the way they are in Philadelphia — were filled with clichés, rarely allowing outsiders to get past his first line of defense. His teammates saw a different player.

"He's not like that," said Sermon, who joined the Eagles this season as a reserve running back. "When he's away from it, he's kind of an old-school, reserved dude."

Sermon and Hurts used to drive every week to a soul food restaurant 30 minutes north of campus. Those laugh-filled drives, Sermon said, are some of the best memories of college as the two friends who became NFL teammates were just college students with a dream.

"I don't even know how we found it," said Sermon, as soul food restaurants aren't on every corner in Oklahoma. "It was definitely hard to find. But once we went there one time, we went there a lot after."

Hurts, a few months after sitting in the grass with Basquine, invited the receiver over to his apartment. Hurts had an old Xbox 360 and NCAA

Jalen Hurts competed for and secured the Sooners' starting quarterback job after his high-profile transfer to Oklahoma. (AP Images)

Football 14, the last edition in the video game series that halted production when Hurts was a freshman in high school.

The game in the quarterback's apartment had current rosters — "He had them updated somehow," Basquine said — as Hurts was Oklahoma's quarterback and Basquine was one of the receivers. They played Oklahoma vs. Oklahoma, pitting their virtual selves against each other.

Hurts, who came off at times like a cyborg created to play football, was just a college kid playing as himself in a video game.

"He's going to dispute it, but let's say I came out on top," Basquine said. "He's his own person. He does a good job of keeping things to himself, but once you get into that inner circle, he's a good dude. He knows how to have fun."

LeBron Special

Riley sat next to Hurts on the flight home from Kansas State, telling the quarterback that perhaps he should address the team and reiterate some of the things the coach told the players in the locker room. Hurts said he would do so after the team landed in Oklahoma City.

"I thought he meant, 'We'll bus back to the facility and I'll talk to them,'" Riley said.

And there was Hurts on the tarmac, a group of 70 players hanging on his every word as he made them believe their season wasn't finished.

"He started talking and it just fired us up," said offensive lineman Tyrese Robinson, now a member of the Eagles practice squad. "And we were just ready for that next practice on Monday."

The Sooners won three straight games, answering the quarterback's challenge as they rolled into Oklahoma State for their rivalry game. A win and they'd advance to the conference championship game.

Riley had installed a new play that week — LeBron Special — that was similar to the Philly Special run a year earlier by Doug Pederson in the Super Bowl.

Hurts took the snap, tossed it in the backfield to receiver CeeDee Lamb, who pitched it to Basquine before the former baseball player fired a pass to Hurts in the end zone. They practiced it before leaving for Oklahoma State and the staff told the players they would run it if the right situation arrived.

Here it was: Sooners on the 4-yard line ahead by three points in the first half. Basquine had thrown a pass earlier that season, but this was different. It was windy and the players were jammed together close to the goal line. And then they had to wait for a commercial break to run the play as Riley's LeBron Special would be the first play of the second quarter.

"I'm like, 'Oh my goodness. Lord, please let me throw this ball accurately,'" Basquine said.

The play went exactly as they practiced. Hurts, the player who needed to be less robotic, stood alone in the end zone as a wide receiver threw him a pass. Oklahoma's free-flowing offense was another win closer to reaching the College Football Playoff as the team answered the challenge of "So what? Now what?" on the tarmac from the quarterback who made himself their leader.

"He cared about everyone on the team from scout players to the top guys," Robinson said. "He could have been selfish, but he always cared about the team. That's how he's always been." ■

Under head coach Lincoln Riley, Jalen Hurts adopted a more free-flowing approach at Oklahoma and finished the season as the Heisman Trophy runner-up. (AP Images)

Off and Running

Jalen Hurts shows that Carson Wentz was Eagles' biggest problem

December 13, 2020 | By Marcus Hayes

As it turns out, it wasn't the offensive line. It wasn't the coach. It wasn't the roster, and, somehow, it wasn't even the defense.

It was Carson James Wentz.

Because everything changed with Jalen Alexander Hurts. The defense played well, Miles Sanders ran for 115 yards and two touchdowns, and the offensive line improves, but Hurts, in his first professional start, was the biggest component in ending the Saints' nine-game winning streak and the Eagles' four-game skid, 24-21.

When I asked him if he wished he'd benched Wentz earlier, coach Doug Pederson refused to directly answer.

"Jalen was a part of it," Pederson said. It was one of his half-dozen, half-hearted evaluations of Hurts' transcendent performance. "I thought there were some good things. ... This win today is not about one guy."

Wrong. It was. As in previous games, there were tons of injuries, tons of penalties and mistakes, tons of bad play calls, and worse coaching decisions.

Jalen Hurts minimized all of the miscues. That's what good quarterbacks do.

That's where Wentz has failed.

Pederson knows that. Then, Pederson failed Hurts after the game. Pederson, incredibly, wouldn't even name Hurts the starter for next week's game in Arizona. Why? Because Pederson cared more about not hurting Carson Wentz's feelings than he cared about thanking the player who saved his own job.

Pederson's players didn't care about Carson's tender feels.

"He's a natural leader ... We looked like a complete team," said Sanders, who enjoyed the most dynamically productive game of his two-year career. "When you have a quarterback that can run the ball effectively ..."

"The guy's a winner," said first-round rookie receiver Jalen Reagor, who had a second big play from Hurts' hand in as many weeks. "He knows how to play."

That's why Hurts was a second-round pick in April, and a controversial one, considering Wentz was inked for five more years and the Eagles had other needs. The controversy amplified when Hurts replaced Wentz as the Eagles' starter Sunday. Wentz dragged the Eagles down to a 3-8-1 record, losers of their last four. Wentz was, by every measure, the worst quarterback in the NFL: passer rating, interceptions, total turnovers, sacks, confidence.

Carson Wentz watches from the sideline during Jalen Hurts' first NFL start, a 24-21 win over the New Orleans Saints. (Yong Kim / Staff Photographer)

Independent of other failures — roster depth, age, play-calling, injuries — Wentz actively lost games.

Pederson finally replaced Wentz with Hurts in the fourth quarter of the previous week's loss to the Packers, then switched starters the next night. He won't admit it, but he was three weeks late.

Hurts on Sunday: No interceptions, one turnover (a late, careless fumble), no sacks taken, and tons of muted swagger. It's the sort of swagger you'd figure a national champion Heisman Trophy finalist would have.

Against the first-place Saints and their No. 1-ranked defense, Hurts led the Eagles to a 17-0 halftime lead. He did so with aplomb. He led a 53-yard, fourth-quarter drive to make it 24-14. He looked like a faster, smarter, more polished version of rookie Donovan Jamal McNabb.

We haven't seen poise like this since Nicholas Edward Foles.

Greatness is contagious

You've heard the adage about how good quarterbacks make the players around them better? Well, Alshon Jeffery had two catches in four games before Sunday. He caught a TD pass early in the second quarter Sunday. Sanders averaged 49.3 rushing yards and had no touchdowns during the Eagles' four-game losing streak. Sanders gained 96 yards with a TD by halftime Sunday. Wentz led the league with 50 sacks taken this season, 18 of them in the last four weeks.

Understand: Jalen Hurts faced all the same challenges Carson Wentz faced.

Hurts played behind a 12th different offensive-line combination in 13 weeks — a line playing without injured Pro Bowl regulars Jason Peters, Lane Johnson, and Brandon Brooks. Hurts played without DeSean Jackson, with old, slow Jeffery, with diminished tight end Zach Ertz. Hurts played with a roster of backups compiled by embattled Howie Roseman. Hurts ran a game plan compiled and called by embattled coach Doug Pederson.

Only one thing changed Sunday.

Carson Wentz sat.

Wentz is no lost cause. He's big, smart, has a strong arm, has won games, and he's only 27, with five seasons in the league. He also is, grading on a $128 million contract curve, the worst player in the National Football League. And by far the worst player on the Philadelphia Eagles.

On Sunday, if Hurts wasn't the best, he was the most valuable.

He gained 106 rushing yards on 18 carries, only the second quarterback in NFL history to crack 100 yards in his first start. The other: reigning MVP Lamar Jackson.

He completed 17 of 30 passes for 167 yards and a touchdown. And he won a must-win game, kept the Eagles in the NFC East title chase, and did so against the best team in the conference. He wasn't perfect, and he knows it.

"A lot of money we left on the table out there," Hurts said, utterly resplendent in a simple white shirt, the collar fastened with a contrasting black stud. He looked like straight cash, as he repeated, "A lot of money."

Which is exactly what a money player would say.

As a senior at Oklahoma he passed for 3,851 yards, eighth in the NCAA, with 32 touchdowns,

Jalen Hurts waits to throw during warmups ahead of his first start. (Yong Kim / Staff Photographer)

which was 11th, and eight interceptions for a 191.2 passer rating, which was second. He also rushed for 20 touchdowns, which ranked seventh. His 53 total touchdowns ranked second; Joe Burrow, the No. 1 overall pick, threw 60 TD passes. His 1,298 rushing yards ranked 18th. This was not an aberration.

This is the new norm.

It wasn't as if Hurts got lucky. It wasn't as if Hurts got calls. He was, simply, better than Wentz. He made good throws. He made strong runs. He made good decisions.

Hurts scrambled 5 yards to convert a third-and-4. He ran 15 yards to convert a second-and-11 out of his own end zone. In the final minute of the first half he scrambled for 24 yards, then for 16 yards, which set up a short field-goal try. He converted third-and-5 late in the third quarter that helped his injury-depleted defense rest; it forced a turnover on the next Saints possession.

Hurts ran better than Wentz because he's a better runner; Wentz has never run for more than 65 yards. Hurts ran a 4.59-second 40-yard dash in February. Wentz once ran a respectable 4.77, but that was more than five years ago, and that was before knee and back injuries, 179 sacks, and a playoff concussion.

Hurts also ran through Marcus Williams on a shotgun quarterback keeper. Of course, Hurts squatted nearly 600 pounds in college.

Carson Wentz did not squat 600 pounds.

The difference in demeanor between Hurts and Wentz was overwhelming, even to a purportedly neutral entity. The Fox broadcast played Demi Lovato's "Confident" when it went to commercial as officials reviewed what should have been an Ertz reception.

On third-and-9 at the Eagles' 40, against a four-man rush, facing no spy, he didn't take a sack. He just threw it away. The Eagles punted. The Saints got the ball at their 20. Like football is supposed to be played.

Hurts just missed Reagor deep to start a series. Two plays later, on third and-7, he quietly stood in the pocket and hit Reagor in stride for a 39-yard catch-and-run.

Facing fourth-and-2 at the Saints' 15, he gave Jeffery a chance to make a catch. Jeffery did. Touchdown. He ate a roughing-the-passer hit on the play.

Got up. Walked away.

As we noted last week, the Saints' defense was first in the league in yards allowed (288.8 per game), fourth in points allowed (20.1), second in run defense (76.1), and fourth in pass defense (212.8). It was tied for third in sacks (36) and seventh in interceptions (13).

The Saints complicated the game in the second half with a barrage of blitzes but considering Hurts had taken just 59 total snaps before Sunday, a measure of befuddlement should be expected. The Eagles' defense had lost six of its top 13 players by the early fourth quarter, so the Saints' comeback path was cleared. The comeback didn't happen.

Hurts outplayed his profile match, run-first backup Taysom Hill. But more than anything, Hurts made Wentz a postscript to the 2020 season.

Finally. ■

Jalen Hurts is congratulated by Carson Wentz after scoring against the Saints. (Yong Kim / Staff Photographer)

Fully Focused

Jalen Hurts just wants to be a coffee bean

December 25, 2020 | By Jeff McLane

Jalen Hurts spoke about as much as a coffee bean when he first joined the Eagles. Some of his teammates and coaches didn't know what to make of his quietness. Did he have a personality? Was he being arrogant? Or was he like most rookies: overwhelmed?

But as time passed, most of Hurts' new colleagues came to the realization that he didn't talk much because he was rigorously learning how to become an NFL quarterback. He was too focused on the task at hand to suffer through idle conversation.

Diligent has often been the word Eagles coach Doug Pederson and his assistants have used around the NovaCare Complex to describe Hurts when others may question his supposed aloofness.

"Jalen, he doesn't get real high and he doesn't get real low," Pederson said, using an oft-repeated quarterback cliche, but one that seemingly applies here. "He just kind of flat lines just a little bit. And that's a good thing. His blood pressure stays pretty low for the most part."

But Hurts has gradually revealed more of himself, both privately and publicly, especially since becoming the Eagles' starter earlier this month. Some of it has been unavoidable. The rookie spoke to Philadelphia-area reporters only twice before he replaced the benched Carson Wentz against the Packers.

Hurts still comes off as robotic in interviews, but in some ways that's really his demeanor. A coach's son, he's been conditioned to do and say as told, and that can often lead to him borrowing the phrases of his coaches.

This week, it was Nick Saban's "rat poison," an expression the Alabama coach has used to describe the outside distractions fans and media can create. Last week, it was "coffee bean," a metaphor he used to explain his approach to leadership.

The latter phrase came from a self-help allegory. Hurts also used it in August 2019 when he won the starting job at Oklahoma. The proverb goes: Life is difficult and can feel like a pot of boiling water. A carrot softens in the pot. An egg hardens. But the coffee bean melts and transforms the water.

Hurts has been tossed into another quarterback controversy. Will he wilt? Will he become more rigid? Or will he overcome the challenge by using his inner strength to alter his circumstances?

Jalen Hurts runs to the Eagles' end zone to celebrate a touchdown against the Arizona Cardinals. (Yong Kim / Staff Photographer)

The 22-year-old Hurts has started only two games — a win and a loss — but he has already created positive change.

"Impacting people, bringing people up around me," Hurts said when asked why he doesn't seem to get rattled. "Always take somebody with you and create that camaraderie, that community. And all those things, all those characteristics, they're contagious.

"Just trying to be a coffee bean."

Quiet confidence

It's unclear if Hurts read the book or simply was told the proverb. But he apparently has a handful of sayings he falls back on, some analogies he has concocted himself to the amusement of some with the Eagles.

"I guess it's a way to uplift the guys around me," Hurts said. "And that's all I try and do with those sayings, I guess. Bring somebody with me and have positive energy, always being optimistic in anything that we do."

His future is uncertain. But he has Sunday at the Cowboys, the season finale the following week against Washington, and maybe a playoff appearance, to make the case that he should be the starter next season.

Philly's as tough a sports town there is, but Wentz's struggles have had many fans welcoming the possibility. Most overlooked Hurts' fashion faux pas when the Houston-area native wore Astros garb to his first Zoom interview as the starter, however manufactured the outrage might have been.

The locker room may be even more difficult to win over, and by most appearances, the players have accepted Hurts. Younger skill position players, like receivers Quez Watkins and Greg Ward, have seemingly been the closest to him. But numerous players have highlighted his outward confidence more than any other characteristic.

Tackle Jordan Mailata called it a "swagger." Running back Miles Sanders said his conviction was "through the roof."

Veterans like defensive tackle Fletcher Cox and center Jason Kelce have been outspoken in support of Wentz. But Kelce, for instance, has given further voice to Hurts' coffee bean conceit.

"He's got great confidence in himself first and foremost which breeds off into other guys," Kelce said. "He's a little bit quieter, but then again most rookies are, especially when you're just trying to learn and figure out where your place is on the team and what you're doing."

The pandemic restrictions haven't helped relationship-building this season. Most of the player interaction has been on the field. Even amongst the position groups, it's been difficult to establish camaraderie. Wentz and Hurts have admitted as much.

Hurts was able to drift under the radar once the team reported for training camp in August, and not just because of his quiet demeanor. He was originally slotted as the third quarterback behind Wentz and Nate Sudfeld, and many of the coaches didn't yet know what they had.

Pederson, quarterbacks coach Press Taylor, and senior offensive assistant Rich Scangarello worked primarily with Wentz through the first month. Marty Mornhinweg, who was brought back to the Eagles as a senior consultant, and who Hurts recently called a "wise old owl," focused more on the rookie.

Been there, done that

Pederson didn't even activate Hurts for Week 1. And when he dressed for Week 2, it had more to do with bringing another dimension to a struggling offense than it did with promoting him to the backup role.

But there were voices at the NovaCare that called for more Hurts plays and increasingly saw him as a threat to Wentz. He kept his head down having been on the flip side at Alabama. Hurts famously lost his job at halftime of the national championship game.

He may have been benched, but he celebrated the Crimson Tide's title as much as his replacement, Tua Tagovailoa. Hurts was prepared by his father, Averion, who coached him in high school at Channelview, a town east of Houston near the Gulf of Mexico, for such moments.

"Being a coach's kid, I've been around football a real long time," said Hurts, whose older brother, Averion, Jr. also played for their father. "And I'm very fortunate and blessed to say that because not a lot of people experience the things that I did growing up. Being in a fieldhouse and all of those things.

"My dad, or even other coaches around me, always said, 'Anybody can lead. They may lead by example [rather than words].' I just want to earn the respect of my teammates."

Hurts did in Tuscaloosa for the way he handled his demotion. He was reinserted the following season while Tagovailoa was injured and Alabama won the SEC championship. But it was back to the sideline for the BCS playoffs and he transferred to Oklahoma for his final college season.

He came in and positively affected another new environment as the Sooners made the playoffs and he finished second in Heisman Trophy voting. Having been through those travails, Hurts came to the Eagles battle tested and hasn't had to playact to get others to follow his lead.

"You're not a pretender. You're not faking it," defensive end Brandon Graham said. "People see the work you put in and now they see you produce on the field and then people start to respect you even more. You get that respect and then eventually you become a leader without even knowing it because people want to be where you are.

"Sometimes some people run from it and some people don't."

Hurts had to be somewhat anxious in his first start vs. the Saints. Sanders said that he had trouble relaying one of Pederson's verbose West Coast offense calls in the huddle early in the game.

"He had to calm himself down," Sanders said. "He didn't rattle. We didn't rush over him. ... He took a deep breath and he said the play. It was like a play with like a whole bunch of the same letters."

But it's been relatively smooth sailing since. And Hurts has gradually come out of his skin and become more vocal. Pederson mentioned the way he tried to fire up the team on the sideline in Arizona. But in individual moments he may also have an aphorism.

"I can talk to him about anything besides football, anything outside of football, and he's gonna hit me with some motivation," Watkins said. "And I might not be trying to hear it at the moment, but it's always helpful.

"He's an uplifting person."

Just like a coffee bean in hot water. ∎

Next Man Up

Carson Wentz trade clears the path to start Jalen Hurts ... for now

February 18, 2021 | By EJ Smith

It's apparently Jalen Hurts' time.

After agreeing to trade Carson Wentz to the Indianapolis Colts Thursday, the Eagles have moved back into the swath of teams searching for a franchise quarterback. Unless Howie Roseman and Co. decide to use their first-round pick on the position in April's draft, Hurts will be the first signal-caller with the chance to lock down the job.

As it stands, the former Oklahoma and Alabama star is the only quarterback on the roster under contract, with Nate Sudfeld again going into free agency. A lot can change from now until the start of training camp, but the decision to move on from Wentz should set up Hurts to enter next season as The Guy.

The Eagles' messaging around Hurts this offseason had been mostly even-handed with praise for Wentz and Hurts, but new head coach Nick Sirianni said he considered Hurts a "top-notch" quarterback.

"We have two quarterbacks, Carson Wentz and Jalen Hurts, that are top-notch," Sirianni said. "A lot of teams don't have any. Just really excited to work with both of them."

Eagles owner Jeffrey Lurie had a similar sentiment last month, calling both players "really interesting assets."

"A coach is going to have an ability to fix what he feels is necessary in our offense and have a potential star in Carson and a potential star in Jalen," Lurie said Jan. 11 after Doug Pederson's firing. "That gives us an asset, also, so that if we end up deciding on one someday, the other is a really good asset."

The first year of Hurts' career was a strange one. The Eagles surprisingly had taken him in the second round of last year's draft with the idea that he'd serve as Wentz's low-cost backup, with the upside to become trade bait if he developed into a starting-quality quarterback. The plan obviously backfired, as did Roseman's claim that he wanted the team to be a "quarterback factory." Instead, Hurts' presence will allow the team a cleaner transition from Wentz after the 28-year-old had the worst statistical season of his career, leading to his benching.

Hurts, 22, started the last four games of the year and had mixed, albeit promising, results. He completed 52% of his passes and threw six

Jalen Hurts was reunited with Carson Wentz as the Eagles beat the Commanders 24-8 in 2022. (Monica Herndon / Staff Photographer)

touchdowns to four interceptions in an offense that was dysfunctional and beset with injuries all year. His completion rate over expectation was minus-3.4%, one of the lowest in the league, although it was an improvement over Wentz's minus-4.1%.

Hurts' running ability gave the Eagles' stagnant offense a spark. In his first start, he rushed for 106 yards and led the Eagles to an improbable win against a top-ranked New Orleans Saints defense. That was his lone win in his four games as the starter, something he said he needed to improve on during his year-end news conference last month.

"I care about nothing but winning. I've been so invested in doing that," Hurts said. "Nothing else matters. How can I grow into the player I know I can be? What does that look like? Who's around me? Who's going to help me get there? That's where my head is. I'm all about growth. I'm all about learning. And I just want to continue to grow as a player and help this team. That's where my head has been these last four weeks. I'm very appreciative of this opportunity and I want to take advantage of it. I'm all about how can I help this team get to where we want to be."

Hurts seemingly won over much of the Eagles' locker room throughout the year with his even-keel personality. In college, he had quickly become the face of two prominent college football programs, first as a freshman starter at Alabama and eventually as a transfer at Oklahoma.

Several Eagles players, including receiver Greg Ward and running back Miles Sanders, called Hurts a "natural leader" once he took over as the starter.

"He's a playmaker, a natural-born leader," Ward said after the Saints game in December. "He went out there and showed that, he made plays, and he made plays on his feet and in the air, and he had that spark, and we all rallied behind him and came out with the win."

Even with his standing in the locker room and the promise of his rookie season, there's still a chance Hurts' path to next season's starting job will grow murkier by summer. According to an Inquirer report, the Eagles will consider drafting a quarterback with the sixth overall pick in April. They could also bring in a free agent, although it's worth noting the team now has a league-record $33.8 million in dead salary-cap money allocated at the position in the aftermath of the trade.

This year's class features a handful of high-rated quarterback prospects, including Clemson's Trevor Lawrence, BYU's Zach Wilson, Ohio State's Justin Fields, and Trey Lance from North Dakota State, Wentz's alma mater. Lawrence is virtually guaranteed to go to the Jacksonville Jaguars with the first pick, but the Eagles could be in a position to get one of the other three. ∎

Jalen Hurts talks with then-coach Doug Pederson after seeing his first snaps against the Green Bay Packers in 2020. (David Maialetti / Staff Photographer)

Securing His Place

The Eagles don't need Jalen Hurts to be the next Randall Cunningham. They just need him to be him.

December 28, 2021 | By Mike Sielski

Jalen Hurts arrived at Lincoln Financial Field on Sunday morning having made an interesting wardrobe choice, one that revealed that he saw himself on a particular continuum of Eagles quarterbacks. He walked into the stadium wearing a retro Randall Cunningham jersey, white with Kelly green embroidery, and he donned the jersey again for his press conference following the Eagles' 34-10 rout of the Giants. Why the Randall jersey? Hurts was making a statement, and he wasn't shy to say so.

"One of the greatest and obviously an icon here," he said. "I always talk about how much it means to be able to play for this organization, knowing the great dual-threat quarterbacks I've had come before me: Mike Vick, [Donovan] McNabb, 5, and Randall Cunningham. I just want to play at a high level and make them proud."

There have been moments this season when comparing Hurts to that trio would have seemed perfectly appropriate, and there have been moments when it would have seemed completely ridiculous — and often it was appropriate and ridiculous in the same game. Cunningham was an NFL MVP, the league's "ultimate weapon," according to a memorable Sports Illustrated cover. McNabb had an MVP-caliber season in 2004 and shepherded the Eagles to five NFC championship games and a Super Bowl. And Vick's accomplishments here surpassed both: He resurrected his career and his life and at last developed, however briefly, into the spectacular passer/runner he could and should have been years earlier.

At their best, those three were genuinely great players. No one would or could argue Hurts has been a great quarterback for an extended period this season, or even for more than consecutive quarters. Take Sunday. Just as he had been just five days earlier, against Washington, he was careless with the football early on, trying to force a pass that was nearly intercepted, then taking a sack and losing a fumble. He had Dallas Goedert wide open in the end zone for a sure touchdown on a broken coverage by the Giants. Though both he and coach Nick Sirianni said that Hurts' progression of reads on the play didn't allow him to see Goedert, it seems impossible that Patrick Mahomes, Tom Brady, or a quarterback closer to their level wouldn't have found a way to get Goedert the ball.

Yet just as he did five days earlier and has done often, Hurts recovered to play better later; in

Jalen Hurts looks to pass during the Eagles' 2021 win against the Giants at Lincoln Financial Field.
(Tyger Williams / Staff Photographer)

the second half, he completed 10 of his 12 passes, including two for touchdowns.

"When he plays good, the offense rolls," Sirianni said, "Just a credit to Jalen to bounce back and play that good second half, because that's what good teams do. They find a way to win."

Because Hurts' status with the Eagles is shrouded in so much uncertainty, because every fine play he pulls off or every mistake he makes seems a referendum on his long-term viability as the team's starting quarterback, it's easy to judge him by a different standard from another quarterback on firmer footing. Already, for example, Hurts has thrown as many touchdown passes in his first full season as a starter, 16, as Carson Wentz did in his, and his yards-per-attempt average is higher than Wentz's was in his rookie year, 2016. More, even if the Eagles lose their final two games, at FedExField against Washington and at home against the Cowboys, Hurts' record as a starter this season would be 7-9, which was Wentz's record in '16.

Those statistics don't mean that Hurts has Wentz's arm strength or size — because he doesn't — and citing a quarterback's win-loss record can be fraught with yeah-buts and eye tests and missing context. But these facts do highlight the grace period afforded to a first-round pick merely for being a first-round draft pick, a grace period that Hurts, if you look at his season as a whole, would appear closer to earning, even as a second-rounder drafted to be a backup.

The Eagles are 8-7 and on the cusp of a postseason berth, and if Hurts gets them into the playoffs — especially if he does so now, on a

sprained ankle that hampers his ability to be his customary threat to run — are his limitations really reason enough for the Eagles to start over this offseason by drafting, trading for, or signing a new starting quarterback?

A first-round pick gets the presumption of improvement. He gets the chance to move past his fumbles and forced throws and bad plays. Given the meager expectations for Hurts and the Eagles entering this season and given their results so far, when does he get the same benefit of the doubt? Should he get that same benefit of the doubt?

"It's a well-rounded question, but I'll tell you honestly: I stay in the moment with everything," Hurts said. "Everybody has goals. Everybody has dreams and things they want to accomplish. We put so much work into this. So there are big dreams and big goals that we want to achieve, but right now, in this moment, I'm happy."

It's a moment no one should look past. No, Hurts hasn't been Randall Cunningham or Donovan McNabb or Michael Vick. He hasn't matched the measure of those quarterbacks' greatest days, not yet, maybe not ever. But he has helped put the Eagles in a position few thought they'd be in, and if he can summon the best version of himself, this season will be considered a success, and he'll come closer to securing his place as their starting quarterback. He has two weeks, starting Sunday in Landover. ■

Before and after the win, Jalen Hurts sported a retro Randall Cunningham jersey, a nod to one of the dual-threat quarterbacks who preceded him in Philadelphia. (David Maialetti / Staff Photographer)

'It'll Still Eat at Him and You'll Never Know'

The playoff struggles that led Jalen Hurts to his first NFL postseason

January 15, 2022 | By Jeff McLane

When college recruiters visited Channelview High School to meet Jalen Hurts for the first time, his father and coach, Averion, would sometimes bring into his office the Fighting Falcons offensive line.

"You'd have this 5-[foot]-6 kid, 5-8 kid. We had one that was 6-foot at the time," Channelview offensive coordinator Byron Henderson said. "And Averion would be like, 'I want you to understand these are the guys that are blocking for him. So everything that he's doing, I want you to see what he's doing it behind.'"

Channelview, located just east of Houston, wasn't a Texas 6A powerhouse when the elder Hurts took over the program in 2006. It hadn't made the playoffs since 1993 and it took 10 more years before the Falcons finally did.

The coach got close with his eldest son, Averion Jr., but it would be Jalen, in his senior year, who led Channelview into the postseason for the first time in 22 years. He did so against substantial odds, as his father, in his peculiar way, demonstrated.

But Jalen Hurts never made excuses, according to Henderson. In fact, Channelview's struggles only made the laser-focused young man that much more determined.

"The process was the important thing, and he'd tell his teammates, 'Hey, let's go out here and do it better than we did it before,'" said Bo Davis, the coach who recruited Hurts to Alabama. "I think he thrived on it. I don't think the losing was a pitfall. He just pushed himself harder and the people around him harder to be successful."

Henderson, also Channelview's quarterbacks coach, Davis and others who were around Hurts in high school aren't surprised he helped guide the Eagles to the playoffs in only his first full season as an NFL starter. They aren't shocked he has rebounded from considerable setbacks in college and the pros, because they saw it firsthand.

When Channelview met powerhouse Manvel in the first round of a bi-district playoff game in 2015, few gave the program a chance. Manvel had around a dozen Division I recruits. Channelview had two, and one was Hurts, who committed to Alabama that June. He might have been the best player on the field, but it takes more than one in football.

Manvel scored the first 47 points and won going away, 71-21. The Mavericks had their share of dynamic moments, especially against an undersized opponent. But what stood out most about Hurts' performance, coaches from both sides said, was his

In his first full season as an NFL starter, Jalen Hurts led the 9–8 Eagles to the playoffs. (Yong Kim / Staff Photographer)

effort and the blow he delivered to a defender in the fourth quarter when the outcome was all but settled.

Asked on Wednesday what he learned about himself competing in his first playoff game, Hurts declined to answer the question.

"What are we getting at with this?" he said, before moving on to the next question.

Henderson said he knew where Hurts was coming from.

"It'll still eat at him and you'll never know," Henderson said. "I'm not comparing him to Michael Jordan, but if you know anything about Michael Jordan, he uses everything as motivation. … It's the same with Jalen. He feels if he takes a moment off, or a moment to reflect, then it's going to deter him from moving forward.

"So he has to have those internal motivations to keep his fire lit to move forward. And I think that's what those games do for him."

Hurts' sights are set solely on the wild-card playoff matchup Sunday at the Buccaneers. The Eagles aren't anywhere near the underdog Channelview was six years ago, but Tampa comes in as an 8-1/2-point favorite with quarterback Tom Brady making his 46th start in the postseason.

The 23-year-old Hurts, who will be the youngest starting playoff quarterback in team history, may not have the 44-year-old Brady's experience. But since his last high school game he played in the biggest "knockout" games at the collegiate level.

"I've been on some very big stages," Hurts said. "I think all of those things have kind of helped me."

He had successes and failures, and sometimes both in the same game, but Hurts has proved resilient. He was trained to be that way. Averion

Hurts coached his son hard to strengthen his mental toughness. He had him power-lift to make him strong enough to withstand the hits.

The former offensive lineman coached him the only way he knew how.

"He wanted Jalen to be tough," said Davis, who first met Averion Hurts when they both coached at Houston-area schools. "And so he groomed him like an O-lineman that you would expect as a former O-lineman dad to do with his son."

Henderson handled more of the particulars of playing quarterback. Hurts was taught to have a short memory. Don't wallow in the last play, the last game, and the last season. He's shown that same resiliency this year. But that doesn't mean he doesn't remember.

When Hurts transferred to Oklahoma, his first game, against Houston, set up a rematch with former Manvel quarterback D'Eriq King. The Manvel defender he ran over, Deontay Anderson, was also a Cougar.

"I haven't forgotten," Hurts said then when asked about his last high school game.

The quarterbacks' roles were reversed with the Sooners heavily favored. Houston never stood a chance. Oklahoma raced out to a 21-0 lead and won, 49-31, as Hurts accounted for more than 500 yards and six total touchdowns.

If Hurts was looking for further Manvel-related inspiration on Sunday, he can look across the field at Raymond James Stadium and see King's backup, Kyle Trask, now the Bucs' third-string quarterback.

Hurts may use his high school adversity as motivation, but he also knew he was destined for more.

"Jalen knew that he would be in the situation that he's in this weekend going into this game against

Jalen Hurts has demonstrated a laser focus and determination at every level of competition, dating back to his high school years at Channelview. (Monica Herndon / Staff Photographer)

Tom Brady," Henderson said. "He knew this in high school. He might not have been playing against Tom Brady, but he knew that he was going to be an NFL quarterback playing in the biggest games."

Nothing affects the guy

Hurts became Channelview's starter in his sophomore year. The Falcons went 1-9 that season. They went 7-4 the next year and upset nearby rival and Texas heavyweight, North Shore, 49-48, when Hurts tossed a 36-yard last-second touchdown.

The playoffs would have to wait another year, but the drought ended with Hurts carrying the team on his shoulders and fans flocking to see the Alabama recruit. Manvel, 37 miles away, knew plenty about the dual-threat quarterback.

"My main concern was him getting loose and running on us," then-Manvel coach Kirk Martin said, "because he's just so big and powerful."

The Mavericks, though, had the athletes to box Hurts in: Power 5 prospects at each level of defense.

"We had some dudes," Martin said.

The size advantage Manvel had up front was significant, and Channelview struggled to move the ball on the ground. Hurts tossed two first-half interceptions. But he kept slinging and threw for 175 yards.

"Jalen was trying to do everything he could to win," said Davis, who was in attendance, "but he just didn't have enough people around him to help him succeed."

Hurts also rushed 22 times for 122 yards and a touchdown, and on one of his last carries, he broke free into the secondary and down the sideline. Anderson, a safety, came over from the post.

"The kid must have thought Jalen was going out of bounds," Henderson said, "and Jalen ran straight through him."

Hurts just stood over Anderson.

"He lowered his shoulder," Martin said.

There was disappointment, of course, but when the final whistle went off, Averion Hurts made the transition from coach to father.

"At that point, nothing needed to be said," Henderson said. "His dad is one of the hardest people on him, even to this day. He got on him throughout the whole game, but being a coach as long as he has, you know you're out-manned, and you know you can only expect one kid to do so much."

A month later, Hurts was at Tuscaloosa already working out and in January he enrolled early. Alabama was the defending national champion and had won four of the last seven titles. Hurts, though, was unfazed and by the second game he won the starting job because, Davis said, "he won the players."

He won games, too, 12 straight as Alabama advanced to the SEC championship game. Hurts made his share of rookie mistakes, but he never batted an eye, at least outwardly.

"With Coach [Nick] Saban, it used to drive him crazy," Davis said. "He'd said, 'Nothing affects the ... guy.' He's like ... armor. He throws an errant pass and he's like, 'OK, I'll get it fixed. I know what I did wrong on it.'

"Most guys come in and they're like, 'Aw, [shoot].'"

Hurts wasn't at his best in the conference title game and then in the national semifinal, but Alabama cruised in both games. In the final in Tampa, the Crimson Tide got into a shootout with Clemson and quarterback Deshaun Watson.

Coaches including Alabama's Nick Saban have noted Jalen Hurts' impenetrable outward demeanor, even in challenging circumstances. (Yong Kim / Staff Photographer)

The Tigers defense allowed few completed passes, but Hurts was undeterred, and his 30-yard rushing touchdown gave Alabama a three-point lead with 2 minutes left. It was more than enough time for Watson to drive Clemson to a touchdown and victory.

A year later, the Tide avenged the loss and beat the Tigers in the semifinals. Hurts' passing inaccuracy caught up to him in the final against Georgia, however, and he was benched at the half for freshman Tua Tagovailoa. Alabama won in overtime.

"There was more going on than just play on the football field," Henderson said. "In the game he got benched, I don't think that he had all of the opportunities to showcase his talents as they did with Tua. I think Tua is a great quarterback, he's a great talent. ... But I can say all that did was fuel even more fire under Jalen."

Tagovailoa remained the starter the next year, but when he injured his foot with 11 minutes left in the SEC championship game against the Bulldogs, Hurts stepped in and tossed and ran for touchdowns as Alabama rallied to win.

"It shows his character," Eagles and former Alabama receiver DeVonta Smith said Thursday. "That's just the type of guy he is. He isn't going to run from any situation. He's going to compete no matter what."

But Tagovailoa returned for the playoffs. Clemson won convincingly in the final, but as Hurts knows as well as anyone, quarterbacks receive far too much credit or blame, especially in the postseason.

Nine days after the loss, Hurts, who wouldn't have to forfeit a year of eligibility because he graduated early, transferred to Oklahoma.

Hurts became a better passer in Norman. The defense-deprived Big 12 helped, but he improved under coach Lincoln Riley. The Sooners beat Baylor in overtime of the conference championship game, but they ran into an LSU buzzsaw in the national semifinal and lost, 63-28.

Prepared for this moment

Averion Hurts, who still coaches Channelview, doesn't do many interviews when his son is the subject. Jalen Hurts has also shied away from talking much about his relationship with his father, other than the "coach's son" dynamic.

"He's done his job, it's time for others to take charge," Henderson said of Averion. "But that doesn't mean he doesn't privately critique Jalen. He critiques him with his preparation and his thought process, not the specifics of the quarterback position."

Henderson and Davis credited Averion for Hurts' unflappable demeanor. His mother, Pamela, also an educator, has influenced his diligence, as well. But Hurts is very much a product of Texas football and of Channelview's struggles, the coaches said.

He has taken every slight, every setback and used it as motivation. Despite his father's best efforts, Hurts had only a few Division I offers his junior season.

"It's not like everybody was knocking down the door," Henderson said. "Averion got coaches to come, but I've always said the perennial playoff teams are going to get the most attention."

Hurts' stock began to rise during offseason showcases, though. Davis was brought in to recruit him because he previously coached at North Shore and knew Averion Hurts when he was at MacArthur High.

"I remembered Jalen watching his brother's games," said Davis, now the defensive line coach at Texas. "But I didn't know he would grow into an athlete like that. He did."

Hurts committed at an Elite 11 quarterback competition in Los Angeles in June 2015, choosing Alabama over Texas A&M and Mississippi State. Davis said he wasn't concerned about his lack of

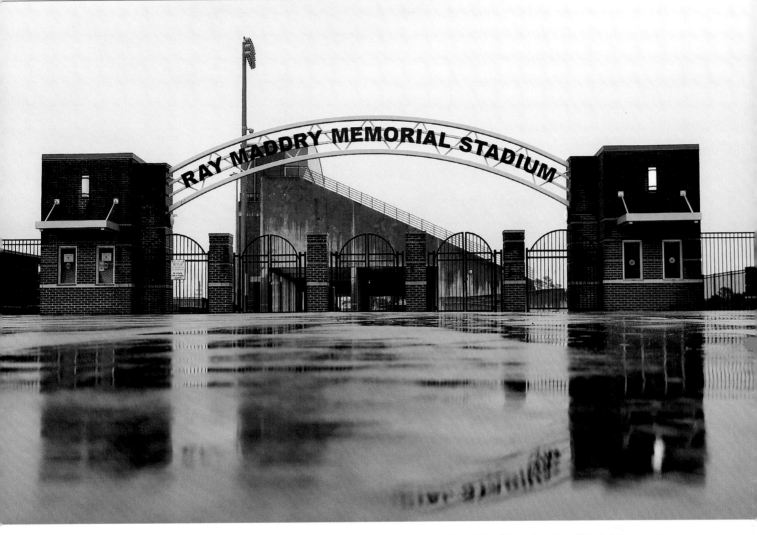

Ray Maddry Memorial Stadium at Channelview High School outside of Houston, where Jalen Hurts played and his dad, Averion, is still the head football coach. (Elizabeth Conley / For The Inquirer)

playoff experience because, he said, "every game in Texas is like the playoffs."

Hurts prepared for every game as if the stakes were that high. Henderson recalled one time after practice, as Hurts was in the weight room working out, he started to pack up to head home to his family for a late dinner. Channelview's upcoming opponent wasn't considered very strong.

"I'm getting my stuff together, Jalen comes in my office and goes, 'Where are you going? I wanted to watch more film,'" Henderson said. "I go, 'Really, Jalen?' Uh, OK, you want to watch, let's go back and watch.'"

They stayed for another hour, according to the coach.

"Jalen helped set the culture here," Henderson said. "We've only missed the playoffs once since he left. ... It didn't take long for the Eagles to get back, did it? Everything in his life has prepared him for this moment.

"From the time he was watching his oldest brother play here, to the time we spent in the back office when he was in high school, everything that has happened to him has prepared him for this moment. And I'm so excited." ∎

'It's My Team'

Jalen Hurts looks ahead to the 2022 season with 'great addition' A.J. Brown

May 4, 2022 | By Josh Tolentino

Jalen Hurts has received public support from his bosses on multiple instances this offseason. During the NFL's scouting combine, Eagles coach Nick Sirianni and general manager Howie Roseman exuded their confidence in Hurts as the team's starting quarterback. Owner Jeffrey Lurie reiterated that point several weeks later at the league meetings, when he described Hurts as "dedicated" and an "excellent leader of men, who gets better every year."

Asked if he feels he's received that message, Hurts offered a pointed reply.

"It's understood," he said. "It's my opportunity. It's my team. It's pretty much what it is.

"This is my team, so I'm ready to go."

Hurts, a 2020 second-round pick, positioned himself to maintain his role as the starter after he helped lead the Eagles to a 9-8 record with an appearance in the NFC's wild-card round. Hurts completed 61.3% of his passes for 3,144 yards with 16 touchdowns and nine interceptions. He also finished as the team's leading rusher with 784 yards and a franchise-best 10 rushing touchdowns by a quarterback in a single season. Hurts was hobbled late in the season by a high-ankle sprain, which required offseason surgery.

"I'm good now; that's all that matters," Hurts said regarding the injury.

Despite Hurts' climb in his first year as the full-time starter, the team conducted due diligence in regard to outside upgrades at the position, especially when considering it possessed three first-round picks at the conclusion of the season. The Inquirer confirmed the Eagles reached out to Russell Wilson and Deshaun Watson's respective former teams, but those talks never progressed as Wilson and Watson landed in Denver and Cleveland, respectively, while Philadelphia moved forward with Hurts.

Hurts insists he doesn't listen to any "rat poison" or outside noise. But team captain Brandon Graham acknowledged Hurts is at least aware of what's being said about him outside of the team-controlled environment at NovaCare Complex.

"I've seen him grow a whole lot," Graham said of Hurts. "Especially through all the adversity he's gone through – he doesn't know if he's going to be the guy.

Jalen Hurts and A.J. Brown have been close friends since high school but did not play together until the Eagles acquired Brown in 2022. (David Maialetti / Staff Photographer)

There's so much talk like 'They're giving Jalen help, this will be his only year to do it because we have a first round next year.' But all the crazy stuff he went through, he's kept a level head. I'm proud of him because all he does is work."

Hurts likely will need to continue to embrace those challenges.

The team's acquisition of star receiver A.J. Brown – Hurts downplayed his efforts, but he surely played a pivotal role in the Eagles' pursuit of Brown considering the strong relationship between the two players – is an indication the Eagles are looking to compete at a high level sooner rather than later. If Hurts regresses in Year 3, the Eagles could pivot next offseason as they possess two first-round picks in a draft class seemingly loaded at quarterback.

"It does feel good [for Hurts] going into the offseason for at least one more year," Graham said. "I believe he's going to maximize everything he needs, too, especially with the new additions. ... He's mature enough to handle it ... because he hasn't showed me he's worried about anything other than proving people wrong."

Hurts will have a chance to accomplish just that with the help of Brown, who is expected to be a dynamic addition to the team's passing offense. During his three seasons with Tennessee, Brown had 24 receiving touchdowns. Hurts and Brown have maintained a close relationship dating to their high school days.

"He's always been an excellent player since I've known him [before] college," Hurts said of Brown. "He's always had the ability to make plays with the ball in his hand, use his body, box out defenders, break tackles. He's a great addition to a great receiver room we have now, and I'm excited."

Hurts has maintained a relatively quiet profile this offseason. Besides appearing at a Sixers game, he hasn't posted much on his social media accounts. Hurts acknowledged he's been training in Southern California, although he declined to delve further. He said his biggest area of concentration was fine-tuning his schedule and approach.

"My young career, I've always been trying to find out what's my [best] way of doing things in the offseason," Hurts said. "It's a holistic approach of taking the next step as a quarterback, whether it be running the offense, taking true command in the weight room and what I'm eating, how much film I'm watching – just practicing great discipline with what I do.

"I had a very unique plan. I tried to challenge myself to do things I've never done. Whether it be watching things on the defense or certain things on tape, working on flexibility. When you play the quarterback position, it's not all about physical ability. It's about mental ability and being able to manage those different situations and lead a team. There's so much that goes into it. I just tried to challenge myself to do that this offseason." ■

Jalen Hurts runs a drill with quarterback coach Brian Johnson during OTAs ahead of the 2022 season.
(Heather Khalifa / Staff Photographer)

THE
BREAKTHROUGH

Off to the Races

Why are the Eagles 5-0? Easy. Jalen Hurts doesn't do dumb stuff.

October 10, 2022 | By Mike Sielski

J alen Hurts holds two weekly press conferences with the media who cover the Eagles, including one session immediately after each game, and they offer an insight into the man who would be King of Philadelphia.

Hurts does not make any jokes during his press conferences. He doesn't engage in playful give-and-take with any of the beat writers or TV reporters. We threaten to feed him "rat poison," after all, and there is no joshing to be done with someone you perceive will do you harm.

No, there is no levity of any kind. There is only Hurts' intense humorlessness and seriousness as he delivers each of his answers, balancing praise of his teammates against his reluctance to say anything too revealing. He could say more, if he chose to, but he doesn't.

What those interactions do reveal is Hurts' ability to be disciplined in a setting in which it would be easy for him not to be disciplined. His words are considered, and he is in control at all times. He isn't glib. He doesn't display any outward anger. He measures what he is about to say or do before he says or does it. No one has yet listened to or walked away from a Jalen Hurts media availability and remarked, Can you believe he said that?

Sometimes a press conference is just a press conference, but in Hurts' case, it is something more. It's an example of a valuable and underrated quality he possesses, one that has helped the Eagles win their first five games this season, one that stood out in their recent 20-17 victory over the Arizona Cardinals. That sense of self-control that Hurts projects whenever he's standing at a lectern or sitting behind a microphone extends to the field, too. He has not been careless or reckless in his play. He has thrown just two interceptions. His INT percentage, 1.3, is tied for fifth-best in the NFL. He has fumbled just twice and didn't lose either one. There are 11 quarterbacks who have fumbled four times or more already this season. He is a coach's son, and so far, it shows.

The most encouraging part of this trend for the Eagles, of course, is that Hurts has protected the ball while still producing big plays. He is averaging 8.5 yards per passing attempt, the second-highest mark in the league. But in the name of being daring, a quarterback often makes the kinds of mistakes

The calm attitude Jalen Hurts displays on and off the field is a steadying presence for the Eagles. (David Maialetti / Staff Photographer)

that hurt his team at best and cripple it at worst. Hurts isn't making those mistakes. When he has made a poor decision or throw this season — his pick-six interception against the Jaguars, for instance, or Jalen Thompson's near-interception for the Cardinals— it has been surprising for its rarity. Patrick Mahomes, Aaron Rodgers, Russell Wilson, Josh Allen: All of them have had their passes intercepted at a higher rate than Hurts. Derek Carr, Tua Tagovailoa, Carson Wentz, Matthew Stafford, Matt Ryan: All of them have interception rates that are at least twice as high as Hurts'.

Sunday was the latest and starkest example of the benefits of Hurts' combination of cautious and assertiveness, and the reason that the example was so stark is that the game was so close. Its outcome came down to a play here, a play there, and the two most consequential sequences demonstrated the contrast between Hurts and Arizona's Kyler Murray. With 4½ minutes left, on third-and-11 from the Cardinals' 36-yard line, Hurts called an audible, dialing up a quick throw to counteract a blitz, and found Dallas Goedert for 16 yards. The first down led to Cameron Dicker's go-ahead field goal.

As calm and commanding as Hurts was, Murray was frenetic on the Cardinals' final possession — reacting, not anticipating. He had Zach Ertz wide open for a long gain and launched a pass so far over Ertz's head that it appeared Murray was throwing the ball away to stop the clock. That error was merely a prelude, of course, to his bigger gaffe: his decision on a second-and-10 scramble, with the Cardinals out of timeouts, to start his give-up slide a yard short of the first-down marker. Had Murray made certain he

got a new set of downs — and he could have made certain — the Cardinals would've had another shot to score a winning touchdown. Instead, they spiked the ball, settled for a field goal, and watched Matt Ammendola's kick sail wide of the right upright.

"I personally have mixed emotions about the game itself," Hurts said afterward. "But we found a way. We found a way."

Why were his emotions mixed?

"As a competitor," he said, "when you have the ball in your hands at the end of a game, you want to take advantage of it and not give the opposition an opportunity to win the game, tie the game, whatever it is. And I don't look at anybody else but myself. I look in the mirror and look at myself and ask myself, 'What could I have done more not to put the team in this position toward the end of the game? How could I have gotten us in the end zone?'"

A commendable sentiment. Jalen Hurts wanted to win his team the game. But he did the next-best thing, and he has been doing it throughout the Eagles' five perfect weeks. He made sure he didn't lose it. ■

The combination of avoiding major mistakes and being selectively aggressive helped Jalen Hurts and the Eagles jump out to a 5-0 start on the season. (David Maialetti / Staff Photographer)

A Hero's Homecoming

Inside Jalen Hurts' Houston legend: Family, football, food, and fantastic finishes

November 3, 2022 | By EJ Smith

Averion Hurts Jr. still gets goose bumps. As he stands under the lights of a rain-soaked high school football field on Tuesday, a train whizzing by disrupts him as he recounts the eight-year-old story of his kid brother Jalen doing something that seemed impossible.

Once the raucous sound subsides, the story that still elicits chills continues: He's back in his dorm room at Kilgore College, listening to a radio broadcast of his dad and brother's game against local powerhouse North Shore, clinging to every word. His brother tosses a deep touchdown pass in the waning seconds, becoming the first quarterback in Channelview High School history to beat the crosstown rival.

"I felt like I was there," Averion Jr. told The Inquirer. "I'm getting the chills just thinking about it now."

Houston is where Jalen Hurts, nicknamed "J Bug" as a kid, was shaped. It is where he first defied the limits put on him even from those who knew him well, by way of obsessively working to improve. On Thursday, the city that forged him will welcome the Eagles quarterback for the first time in his professional career as his team plays the Texans at NRG Stadium.

When he and Averion Jr. visited the stadium formerly known as Reliant as kids, it was hard to imagine Hurts would one day return as a starting quarterback in the NFL and an MVP candidate. But then again, there was a time when Hurts' last-second touchdown pass against the North Shore Mustangs seemed inconceivable as well.

"That was the moment that I knew," Averion Jr. said. "This cat is for real."

'A Hurts thing'

Every once in a while, Jalen Hurts will get a shipment of live crawfish to the Philadelphia area.

The deliveries from somewhere near the Gulf are a way for Hurts to bring a piece of East Houston to his new home. Outside of family, food may be the biggest source of nostalgia Jalen has for his hometown: the Popeye's on Sheldon Road that he'd go to every Tuesday after practice and the Wingstop on Wallisville after games. The chitlins, pig feet, gumbo, and collard greens that his relatives made.

Jalen Hurts returned to his hometown of Houston on Nov. 3, 2022, and the Eagles emerged with a 29-17 victory over the Texans. (Monica Herndon / Staff Photographer)

None reign over the crawfish. The recipe has been passed down two generations from his grandfather, and the Hurts family has become renowned for its cookouts with the crustacean as the main course.

"It's just kind of been this tree," Jalen said. "As a kid, I loved eating crawfish. My dad trained me early, 5 years old, I had to help him in the process of cooking it. I ended up learning how to do it myself. By the time I was in middle school, I was cooking it on my own for the family and different cookouts."

Those who have tried both Jalen's and Averion Sr.'s crawfish mostly agree there are subtle differences between the two. Jalen's early attempts at making it were a good deal spicier than his dad's.

No one is exactly comfortable choosing one cook over the other, though.

"Ima plead the fifth on that one," Averion Jr. said. "I don't want to start any in-home wars."

Jalen's culinary time offers a glimpse of his lighter side. Even those closest to him describe him as "stoic" most often, but cookouts are when he can flash some personality.

There's also convenience in one of the few hobbies he has outside of football: Cookouts keep him at home and out of restaurants or in public, where outside noise can sometimes creep in. Instead, his close friend and former teammate Trey Tutt says Jalen puts on some classic R&B and makes the food that reminds him most of home.

"He's a big old-school cat," Tutt said. "He's singing his favorite old-school jams and making his crawfish. That's a time when you'll see him with his guard down."

The music selection typically ranges from Frankie Beverly and Al Green to Johnnie Taylor and the Isley Brothers.

"It's just a vibe," Jalen said. "Set the mood for the people you're around and just enjoy that time. Especially going back now. I remember my dad would always play his music and we just chilled outside.

"It's in us. That's a Hurts thing, I feel like: Eating crawfish and hanging out. You ask anybody on the east side of Houston, they know that's what we do."

'The spitting image'

There's a silver Ford pickup truck parked right outside the doors of Channelview's field house with a noticeably specific arrangement of logos on the back window.

An Alabama decal sits in the top right corner and an Oklahoma sticker on the opposite side. Each is somewhat symbolically flanked by an Eagles emblem neatly situated on either end of the truck's rear brake light.

The juxtaposition continues once you walk through the double doors into the field house. Along the left wall are displays of noteworthy individuals who once played at the school. Halfway down the collection of photos and trophies, three helmets make up the top shelf and effectively tell the story of Jalen's path to stardom: Two crimson helmets eventually giving way to the midnight green so many in the town have recently adopted.

Opposite the wall of photos, jerseys, and hardware, Averion Hurts Sr. sits in his office with his pickup in eyeshot and his son's Eagles jersey proudly displayed on the back wall.

"There's the head man," said DJ McNorton, a former Channelview standout and current assistant coach as he walks by Averion Sr.'s office.

Like Jalen, Averion Sr. has a tendency to elude the spotlight that has come from his son's storied career on a national stage. The longtime football coach declined to publicly comment, saying he'd rather Jalen and Channelview assistant coaches like McNorton get the "shine" leading up to his son's homecoming.

Their shared aversion of feeding into the outside noise is far from the only similarity between the two men. There's a similarity between them that is instantly noticeable. It is in the way they both talk, the way they have each coined phrases like "keep the main thing the main thing," and how they harp on the importance of staying hyper-focused on the task at hand.

McNorton played with Averion Jr. and first met Jalen when he was a ball boy for his older brother's team. Along with star athlete Jackie Hinton and

Averion Jr., McNorton was one of Jalen's early idols as a kid.

"I wouldn't be where I am without those guys," Jalen said over the summer. "Those are my No. 1 supporters back home because those are the guys that I looked up to. I've said it before, I used to spat my ankles because I saw those guys spatting their ankles."

After playing for Averion Sr. and playing college ball at North Dakota State, McNorton returned to the Channelview sidelines by the time Jalen was in high school. He's spent this year as the pass-game coordinator and wide receivers coach.

"He has the exact same demeanor that you see with Jalen," McNorton said. "That exact same demeanor. Jalen gets it from him. He has that. It may come across as intimidating — I know he can be intimidating when he needs to be — but he's always been great for me. Mentor, coach, all those things."

Being identically wired didn't always result in harmony for the father-son duo, but the main thing was always behind Averion Sr. pushing his son to be "the best version of himself."

"I feel like he has so much love for me, he wanted me to do it right," Jalen said. "So he would get frustrated with me. He wanted me to be the best that I could be, and he was passionate about it. I think we're definitely wise in very similar ways. As I've gotten older, I've just experienced things and I've been able to see things differently.

"At heart, we are the same man," Jalen added. "I'm definitely the spitting image of him."

Some of the foundational elements of Jalen's personality can be traced back to his dad. The stoic disposition and intense focus that Jalen has become known for in Philadelphia is also present in the Channelview field house.

"That's his spitting image," Averion Jr. said, unknowingly echoing his younger brother. "It's kind of annoying sometimes. He'll try to be my dad sometimes. I'll be like, 'Hold on Jalen, I'm big bro, now. I'm big bro.' That's the reason he's in the position that he's in. I don't fault him or hold it against him when he does stuff like that. It's just him."

Eagles coach Nick Sirianni lauded Jalen's ability to stay composed during the ups and downs of a game earlier this season, even pointing to his calm reaction to fans falling out of the stands in Washington as he walked through the tunnel last season.

Former Eagles coach Doug Pederson once told Arizona Cardinals coach Kliff Kingsbury he sometimes had to check Jalen for a pulse during big moments because he takes so much pride in avoiding the ups and downs of games.

"It doesn't matter if he threw an interception or I'm screaming in his face," Sirianni said. "The people in Washington fall out of the stands and almost break his leg, he's pretty unfazed and that's a great quality to have as a quarterback because he's going to be unfazed in the first quarter, he's going to be unfazed in the second quarter, third, fourth."

Even his older brother couldn't always see through the stone face.

"You never know what he's thinking," Averion Jr. said. "You never know what he was feeling. Before he was the star football player, he was that way as a kid. It was frustrating at times."

That demeanor stems from Averion Sr.'s sideline temperament.

"One of the biggest things that I see is both of them have a poise and a confidence about themselves," Tutt said. "You see it a lot with Jalen on Sundays. You see it with his dad on Friday nights. Even when things get tough or things aren't going their way, they're so calm. Nothing ever seems to bother them. They're always in the same atmosphere. They look the same the entire time."

What seemed impossible

Eight years later, people from Channelview are still talking about Jalen Hurts' signature win.

Roughly 20 miles away from NRG Stadium, Jalen and his teammates pulled off what seemed impossible to some: a 49-48 win over local powerhouse North Shore.

It was the type of game that packed a gargantuan 11,000-seat stadium so far past capacity that some people couldn't get seats in the bleachers and had to stand along the perimeter.

"Everybody knew who North Shore was and everybody knew who Jalen Hurts was at that time," McNorton said. "It was an east-side type of showdown so everybody wanted to be there."

Channelview and North Shore are situated less than five miles apart, but the narrative surrounding each school in 2014 and long before stood in stark contrast. Channelview was the underdog led by a four-star quarterback prospect. The school had never beaten its crosstown rival and was surrounded on multiple sides by powerhouses like Baytown, Beaumont, and Port Arthur — each having a significant grip on the area's best players.

North Shore was the juggernaut with a handful of Division I prospects and a track record of making it deep into the state playoffs each year. The team went 11-1 the previous season, outscoring opponents by more than 50 points on four occasions. Channelview was one of those unlucky four, getting blown out, 59-0.

The stakes were even higher than that in October 2014.

Growing up in North Shore's school district but playing for his dad at Channelview, Jalen knew the dynamic as well as anybody. One school was considered the fast track to college football success. The other was considered the lesser.

Jalen watched Averion Sr. and Jr. try twice to make history as the first Channelview team to beat North Shore. They fell short both times, which led to Jalen putting North Shore on the list of teams he needed to beat once it was his turn.

"I took it personal for me and my family," Jalen said. "I live in North Shore. I was supposed to go to North Shore High School."

Down six late in the fourth quarter, Jalen got the Falcons about 40 yards from the goal line with the chance to take one shot at the end zone. On the game's penultimate play, Jalen rolled to his right to evade pressure and threw a prayer to wide receiver

E.T. Giles. The pass bounced off Giles' hands, past two North Shore defenders, and into the grips of Channelview receiver Bryant Valentine in the back of the end zone. The touchdown tied things at 48. The extra point, with Jalen as the holder, put the 2014 Channelview team into the history books.

"It was a game nobody expected us to win against a team that we aren't supposed to win against," Jalen said. "The thing about it was, we believed. … It was surreal. That's something that nobody could take away from us.

"I wish I could go back to those moments and just enjoy them one more time."

Shortly after the final whistle, Jalen found his offensive coordinator and quarterbacks coach, Byron Henderson, whose father died a year earlier. The moment he shared with Jalen still resonates with him.

"He just looks at me and goes, 'Coach, we did it,'" Henderson said. "He embraces me and I just broke down even more. I knew my dad would have been really proud of him, not just us, but him."

Ask almost anyone who has been around Jalen since then and they'll say it's the biggest win of his football career.

Bigger than Alabama's 2018 SEC championship or the Red River rivalry the following season at Oklahoma. Bigger than the Big 12 title and bigger than any of his 16 wins over three years with the Eagles.

Jalen wouldn't go so far, but he did acknowledge it's still a conversation piece whenever he's home.

"I think that's a game that, when I go home where my roots are, they're talking about it," Jalen said. "I think it's all love now because I'm from the east side of Houston at the end of the day. Anybody from the east side, they show love and respect because I never forget where I come from."

Eagles quarterbacks coach Brian Johnson played for Averion Sr. and has followed Jalen's career from the beginning.

"I'll tell him to this day. That's probably the most impressive win that he's had as a football player,"

Johnson said. "If you've ever been to North Shore High School and seen the type of talent and the type of program that they have, they don't lose very often."

The school had plenty of thin years before Averion Sr. took over as head coach in 2008. Tutt was on that 2014 team and is a Falcons assistant coach now as well as a teacher in the school district.

The impact of the North Shore win and the program Averion Sr. has built have redefined the narrative on what's possible for athletes in the district, he says.

"A lot of kids think, just because they go to North Shore and play sports over there, they'll get that Division I scholarship and have a better chance," Tutt said. "He basically shows a kid, in my opinion, that it can be done from here. You don't have to leave Channelview and do it somewhere else. Whatever you want to accomplish, your goals, you can do it right at Channelview."

Juking trees

Looking back, Averion Jr. finally understands.

When he and Jalen were kids, he'd sometimes look over at his younger brother in the backyard, perplexed at the football moves he was executing against the local shrubbery.

"Jalen would always play by himself," Averion Jr. said. "I'd be outside playing basketball and he'd have a football in his hand, trying to juke a tree. Like, 'What are you doing, dude?' It makes sense, you don't question it now. ... I vividly remember him doing that. Running through people's yards, juking trees, spin-moving, dead-legging. Yeah, that's Jalen through and through."

Jalen's talent was evident early on, but those around him didn't know he'd reach the level he has until later. It wasn't until he was midway through high school that most people started realizing he had a chance to be special.

He transferred to Channelview school district in middle school after previously being in North Shore's district. His first year in the new district, he claimed the starting quarterback job over his friend Tutt on the junior high team. The two laugh about it now, but their relationship started off as contentious.

"I was like, 'Man, who is this kid? Who is this dude trying to steal my spot?'" Tutt said. "We'd go to practice every day and he'd throw the ball extremely hard to me — of course, he had a great arm at the time. He was bigger than us as well. He'd throw the ball hard at me and we'd kind of just, you know, share words here and there. It's kind of funny."

Jalen had the size and athleticism to pique interest as a middle schooler, but still hadn't elicited dreams of an NFL future at the position quite yet.

Henderson said Jalen was clearly on pace to be a starter on the varsity team eventually, but there was work to be done to get him ready.

"He was athletic," Henderson said. "He didn't throw the ball very well; I knew that we'd had some work to do. I knew he was going to be our quarterback one day, though."

Once Jalen got to high school, Henderson knew that wouldn't be a problem.

Jalen was playing freshman ball but would pop into the assistant coach's office to ask Henderson for extra coaching after freshman practice was through. If it wasn't on-field work, he'd want to watch film.

Maybe Jalen was just killing time waiting for his dad to drive him home after the coach was through with his evening responsibilities?

"I told him, 'I can take you home,'" Henderson said. "Nope. He wanted to be here. This is where he lived. This was his sanctuary. If he was a basketball player, they'd call him a gym rat. I say he's a field house rat."

It wasn't until he saw how much time Jalen was willing to invest that Henderson realized he needed to reevaluate how good the young quarterback could be.

"Going and seeing a game or two in middle school, you only get a brief showing," Henderson said. "Sitting here, and I've been doing this 25 years, watching him and his work ethic is what made me

know he was going to be special. It was never his talent in the beginning. It was, 'This kid works harder than anyone I've been around.'"

Johnson, then an assistant at Utah, visited Jalen around his junior year. He knew then that Averion Sr.'s kid was wired enough like his dad to get the most out of his talent.

"You could tell that he had that same demeanor that he has now," Johnson said. "Very serious. And you could tell he was going to be a really, really good player. Obviously, he was raw still, he was 15 or 16 years old at the time. You could see him as an athlete, him as a person, him as a player, you could tell he was going to be a really good player."

See you at NRG

Averion Sr. and Jr. both have their schedules cleared on Thursday night when the Eagles will take on the Texans in Houston.

Channelview (7-2) rescheduled its final regular-season game to Friday night because of the occasion. Instead, the school will have a tailgating event at the stadium a few hours before the game.

That's right, a high school football game in Texas was rescheduled for Jalen's homecoming.

Averion Jr., coaching at Summer Creek, had to ask for temporary leave of his typical play-calling duties for freshman games on Thursday night.

"This is a once-in-a-lifetime deal," Averion Jr. said. "Just being able to come back to your city where you know that a lot of people are rooting for you and want to see you do well, it's awesome. Also coming back to the family that's here, it's really big for us."

Jalen and Averion Jr. grew up Texans fans; his godfather Sean Washington led the player development department for the Texans when they were kids and they spent time around Houston's stadium as a result.

"I think going back home and playing in Houston has always been a dream of mine," Jalen said Sunday. "I never had the opportunity to go play in Reliant as a kid, now known as NRG. I spent a lot of time in the Houston Texans facility, my godfather being on staff as a child, and I have a lot of memories at that place, so it'll be exciting."

When he enters NRG Stadium, Jalen will be representing his "new home" in Philadelphia. After wearing a Houston Astros hat and jacket during a video news conference in 2020, Jalen said last week that he's rooting for the Phillies in the World Series.

Still, he'll carry a piece of Houston with him, intentional or not.

"Houston is just in him," McNorton said. "He's Houston all the way, through and through. From the way he talks, the way he dresses. All of it. He's definitely Houston, man."

Jalen added, "It's my music, swag, slang, it's in the soul, too. Special people come from Texas, and special people come from Houston. It's a different pride in being from the city of Houston. I definitely hold a lot of pride in being from that place, knowing the talent that comes from that area, whether it's an artist, a player, a coach, whatever it is, it's the best place in the world." ■

Averion Hurts Jr., Jalen Hurts' older brother, witnessed firsthand the evolution of Hurts into a superstar quarterback. (Elizabeth Conley / For The Inquirer)

Ahead of the Pack

Eagles and Jalen Hurts run all over the Packers as he outduels Aaron Rodgers and sets a franchise record

November 27, 2022 | By EJ Smith

Two years later, things have come full circle for Jalen Hurts.

On Sunday night, the 24-year-old quarterback faced the first team he saw extended playing time against as a rookie and delivered one of the best performances of his career in a 40-33 win over the Green Bay Packers at Lincoln Financial Field.

The progress Hurts has made since that December 2020 evening at Lambeau Field was apparent against Green Bay, as it has been all season.

The Eagles, now 10-1, maintained their lead in both the NFC East and the conference and put together an emphatic, eventful win in prime time.

Hurts boosts MVP case

The early showing from the Eagles' offense had a stark resemblance to the ending of the previous week's win over the Indianapolis Colts.

In lieu of steady offense, the group leaned on Hurts' ability to make things happen with his athleticism in the early going. Hurts reeled off a 24-yard run to complete an improbable third-and-10

with no receivers free on the Eagles' opening drive and followed it up with a 28-yarder on a quarterback draw a few plays later.

"He opened it up today," Eagles running back Miles Sanders said. "I appreciate him for that. It's good to have a quarterback like him when he can just drop back and if you don't see anything and it looks cloudy, he can just take off and get about — not even just 10, 20 yards a gain. That's going to kill a defense and that's going to make them change their play-calling with coverages and stuff like that. It makes them all discombobulated trying to contain all the talent we have on this offense. But yeah, he showed out today."

Hurts had 103 rushing yards in the first quarter alone and finished with one of the most impressive stat lines of his NFL career: 16 completions on 28 attempts, 310 total yards, and two passing touchdowns. His 157 rushing yards set the team's single-game record for a quarterback.

"That's what Jalen does," Eagles coach Nick Sirianni said. "That's where he's special, really special, is where he can make those plays with his feet. To

Jalen Hurts ran wild on the Packers, setting the team's single-game record for a quarterback with 157 yards rushing. (David Maialetti / Staff Photographer)

be in a city like this with the quarterback history that this city has, to set a record for most yards by a quarterback rushing, that's pretty special. There's some unbelievable names that he's following there."

In his first outing against the Packers, he went 5-for-12 for 109 yards, a touchdown, and an interception after replacing Carson Wentz midway through the game. This time around, Hurts outplayed the reigning two-time MVP, leading a resurgent performance for an Eagles offense that hit a rough patch in recent weeks.

Hurts' contributions on the ground were pivotal early in the game, but he also made a handful of impressively placed throws to display the progress he's made as a passer this season. He had a back-shoulder throw to Quez Watkins down the sideline that went for a 30-yard touchdown. On the offense's first series of the second half, Hurts hit receiver DeVonta Smith in a spot that led him away from a Packers defender and allowed him to work upfield.

Especially on a national stage, it was the type of performance that should keep Hurts among the league's candidates for MVP. The Eagles will play more meaningful games and Hurts' performances down the stretch will be the determining factor, but he helped his case Sunday night.

"I've mentioned often the importance of being able to attack teams different ways," Hurts said. "I feel for us as a football team, as an offense, it's like your favorite steakhouse, your favorite, five-star, bougie restaurant that you like to go to. You have your steak of the day, your selection of the day, the chef's selection. I feel like, for us, we can kind of do it all."

Banged-up secondary brings unsung heroes

The Eagles' depleted secondary gave way to a couple of unsung heroes.

Eagles safety C.J. Gardner-Johnson left in the first quarter with a rib injury that held him out for the remainder of the game. Gardner-Johnson, the league leader in interceptions, was slow to get up after colliding with Marcus Epps on a completion to Packers receiver Christian Watson.

Reed Blankenship filled in for Gardner-Johnson and had a pivotal play in the second quarter, baiting and intercepting a pass from Packers quarterback Aaron Rodgers to kill a Packers drive in Eagles territory.

"I saw Aaron Rodgers looking that way and I broke on it," Blankenship said. "I'm surprised he actually threw it, though. That's what surprised me, but I'm happy I got there in time and was able to do something for my team."

Blankenship, an undrafted rookie free agent out of Middle Tennessee State, recently supplanted K'Von Wallace as the extra safety in the Eagles' dime packages and played well in Gardner-Johnson's absence. Gardner-Johnson was carted off.

The Eagles were already without starting slot cornerback Avonte Maddox, who is on injured reserve with a hamstring injury. Josiah Scott, the backup nickel corner, had a pick on the opening series of the game off a deflection from Darius Slay.

Ground and pound

Hurts wasn't the only player dominant in the running game against the Packers defense.

Sanders finished with 143 yards and two touchdowns on 21 carries, marking the first time the Eagles had two rushers surpass 100 yards since Hurts and Sanders did so against the New Orleans Saints in 2020.

Sanders had a couple of explosive runs, including a 15-yard touchdown run in the first

Jalen Hurts greets Green Bay's backup quarterback Jordan Love after dispatching the Packers and Aaron Rodgers, 40-33. (Monica Herndon / Staff Photographer)

quarter and two runs for 20-plus yards on the opening series of the third quarter.

According to Next Gen Stats, Sanders had 49 rush yards over expectation. His two touchdowns brought his season tally to eight. By comparison, Sanders compiled nine touchdowns over the first three years of his career.

Reserve running backs Boston Scott and Kenneth Gainwell combined for 63 yards, including a touchdown from Gainwell. The 363 total yards on the ground were the highest rushing total the Eagles have amassed in 74 years.

After the game, center Jason Kelce wore a "Jeff Stoutland University" T-shirt, crediting the offensive line coach and run-game coordinator for the success on the ground.

"It is a lovely feeling," Sanders said. "I am not going to lie. To beat a good team like that as well with the run game means a lot, too. It shows how much hard work we do each week. I have to give credit not just to the O-line but Coach Stout because he loves running the ball, too, and he has all the confidence in the O-line and running backs especially. That is what we feed off of." ∎

Past and Present

MVP favorite Jalen Hurts shows leadership for Eagles as Carson Wentz gets benched in Washington

December 3, 2022 | By Marcus Hayes

Jalen Hurts lives leadership every second of his life. He leads by example. He leads by inclusion. He leads with love.

Carson Wentz wouldn't know leadership if he worked beside it for three years, and he did, considering Nick Foles and Jalen Hurts were his backups for three of his last four seasons in Philly. He wouldn't know leadership if it gave him his chance in the NFL, and it did; Wentz repaid Doug Pederson by getting him fired.

It was fitting, then, that on the day Jalen Hurts' star rose higher than ever, Carson Wentz's career as an NFL starter likely came to an end.

Hurts broke the Eagles' single game franchise rushing record for quarterbacks last Sunday against the Green Bay Packers with 157 yards, and it's a franchise with the best group of running quarterbacks in NFL history: Michael Vick, Randall Cunningham, and Donovan McNabb. Hurts moved his team to 10-1 for the fourth time in franchise history. Hurts cemented himself as an MVP favorite, along with Patrick Mahomes and a dynamic former college teammate, Tua Tagovailoa.

Wentz forced a trade from Philadelphia to Indianapolis in 2021 after he was benched in Game 12 of 2020. After failing in Indy, Wentz was dumped to Washington in March. Now he's been benched. Again.

He went on injured reserve after Game 6 this season, when the team was 2-4. He watched Taylor Heinicke go 5-1 as his replacement. Wentz was eligible to be activated from IR last week, but the Commanders didn't bother. He might be active Sunday at the Giants — he's been ill this week — but Wentz won't play again this season unless there's an emergency.

Wentz has become a $28 million backup.

He'll probably be holding a clipboard for the foreseeable future, but almost certainly not in D.C. Under his current contract he'd cost the Commanders around $26 million in 2023 and $27 million in 2024.

Meanwhile, Hurts, his unheralded, unappreciated backup in 2020, is looking at a $250 million payday.

Why?

Because, in almost every way, Hurts is the anti-Wentz.

In Hurts' eyes, he's the least important player in

The contrast between Jalen Hurts and former Philadelphia quarterback Carson Wentz has been stark since the latter left the Eagles, with Hurts surging and Wentz benched for the Commanders. (David Maialetti / Staff Photographer)

his locker room. In Hurts' eyes, every coach can help him improve. In Hurts' eyes, nothing matters — not stats, not style, not his Pro Bowl profile — besides winning the next play.

Not the next game. The next play. Winning the game might follow if the next play is won. And he believes that he cannot win by himself; not the next play, or the next game.

Unlike Wentz, he is no hero. Unlike Wentz, he trusts his teammates.

This truth was never more evident than last Sunday night. He'd set the record and he'd won the game, and, in a rare moment of passion, Hurts was willing to reveal how:

"This team enjoys the feeling of winning," he said. "We've talked about some of these things. Execution fuels emotion. You go out there and you talk about something or your coach is on your butt about something throughout the week — 'You need to do it this way,' or 'You need to do it like this,' — you go out and execute it at the most important moment of the game, execution fuels emotion."

Hurts does his job. You do your job. Everybody benefits. Everybody invests. And everybody matters every minute, because no one is promised tomorrow in the NFL.

"We do all of this stuff together. We go to work every day together, we lift together, we run together, we feel pain together, we feel these joyous moments together," Hurts continued. "I know, in a profession where things change all the time, we really want to appreciate the time we are having now and just take advantage of our moments, take advantage of the opportunities when they present themselves, and just play ball the way we want to play ball."

For context:

This was an answer to a question about the offensive line, and how it likes to run-block. But Hurts has one message:

Be your best, and I'll be my best, and if we win, WE win.

Carson loves Carson

This is in jarring contrast to Wentz.

In 2017, as Foles led the Eagles to the Super Bowl after Wentz shredded his knee, Wentz pouted so pointedly that veteran running back Darren Sproles had to reprimand him. In 2018, Wentz ignored certain teammates and bullied his coaches. By 2020, he was angry that the Eagles drafted Hurts in the second round to serve as his backup, and his freelancing on the field and his aloofness off it made his teammates eager for him to leave.

Wentz's main complaint lay in the Eagles' clear lack of faith in him. He admitted that he was convinced he wanted out of Philly as soon as he was benched. So, after halftime of Game 12 in Green Bay — a game with playoff implications and a game Wentz might have had to re-enter — he already was checking out.

That type of selfish pettiness contrasts sharply with Hurts' history.

Nick Saban benched Hurts at halftime of the 2018 national championship game, and Hurts watched backup Tagovailoa lead Alabama to the title. Hurts could have transferred after that season. He didn't. He served as Tua's backup and supporter. Then, when Tagovailoa left the SEC championship game with a leg injury, Hurts entered and led two touchdown drives in a win over Georgia.

Tagovailoa is now an MVP candidate for the Dolphins.

Not unique

Carson cared most about Carson. He's not unique. Most NFL quarterbacks are narcissists. Wentz is just nothing like his successor.

The leadership style of Jalen Hurts has endeared him to his teammates and is a markedly different approach than his predecessor, Carson Wentz. (David Maialetti / Staff Photographer)

Consider how Hurts handled Jordan Mailata in Mailata's worst moment.

Mailata gave up two sacks Nov. 3 at Houston. After the second one, Hurts found Mailata on the sideline. This is the moment where Tom Brady or Peyton Manning would scream at their left tackle. Not Hurts. Quietly, Hurts encouraged Mailata to trust his technique, then told him, "Give me one more second."

Mailata has given up one sack in the three games since, and he averaged an outstanding 77.0 pass-blocking grade, according to profootballfocus.com, his best stretch of the season.

"I like Carson," a former Eagles lineman told me this week, "but I can't see Carson doing that."

That isn't necessarily a criticism of Wentz. Not many quarterbacks would approach that moment the way Hurts did. Wentz likely would have ignored Mailata, but then, so would have Cunningham. McNabb and Vick might would have given Mailata a little pat on the rump.

Jalen Hurts? He made sure he led Mailata.

He made sure he loved Mailata.

Jalen Hurts is just ... different. ∎

'Everything Comes From the Heart'

Jalen Hurts' leadership style through the eyes of Eagles team captains

December 9, 2022 | By Josh Tolentino

Exactly two years ago, the Eagles announced Jalen Hurts as their starting quarterback. After he took over for former starter Carson Wentz, Hurts experienced a tumultuous journey. During his first season as the full-time starter, the former second-round pick guided the Eagles to a 9-8 record with an appearance in the NFC wild-card round.

Heading into the offseason, Hurts received direct feedback from coach Nick Sirianni on teaching points the quarterback later would hammer on. Among them included improving his passing mechanics and his timing in processing his reads and making throws with anticipation and accuracy. The Eagles also aided Hurts by acquiring several playmakers in the offseason, highlighted by the addition of wide receiver A.J. Brown.

With five regular-season games remaining in the 2022 season, Hurts has made dramatic improvements while guiding the Eagles to the NFL's best record (11-1).

The 24-year-old quarterback received conference player of the week honors for the second consecutive week following his excellent performance during the team's 35-10 victory over the Tennessee Titans. Hurts became the first quarterback in league history to throw for 300-plus yards a game after rushing for 150-plus yards in Week 12 against the Packers.

"It's cool," Hurts said of receiving two straight weekly awards. "It comes with a lot of hard work. I definitely acknowledge that. But I'm focused on the Giants. I'm focused on this week. I'm focused on preparing this week."

While Hurts preferred to stay relatively mum regarding his most recent accomplishments, there is a growing buzz surrounding him across the league. Hurts ranks near the top in several of the league's passing statistics, and he has emerged as a legitimate candidate for the NFL's Most Valuable Player award.

The Inquirer interviewed four of the six team captains (outside of Hurts) and received their perspective on Hurts' growth over the last two years.

Right tackle Lane Johnson

"He's been the same since Day 1. He doesn't really say a whole lot. He's quiet; he stays to himself. But when he talks, he's very direct with the way he approaches his message. I think when he says something, it

Jalen Hurts is a man of few words, but when he does speak, there's plenty of meaning and substance behind it. (David Maialetti / Staff Photographer)

always comes with meaning and substance, so that means a lot. Usually after practices or a lift, he'll say something. Usually his message is directed and very to the point. I think he's very levelheaded. He has a very good temperament.

"He knows exactly what he needs to work on, and other guys gravitate toward that. He's always calm. He's just a stoic person. Whatever is thrown at him, he stays levelheaded and consistent with how he's going to handle that adversity."

Cornerback Darius Slay

"Oh, man — he's been a leader ever since he was a rook. He's always had that leadership mentality coming from Alabama. Being a quarterback there for so long, then going to Oklahoma and leading those guys. That's something that he's been doing for a long time. It's like in the back of his mind. It's too easy for him. It's just second nature for him to be a leader. Now, it's a different story with him playing the way that he's been playing. It makes him an even better leader. He's putting the league on notice with how he's leading our team.

"He just carries himself the right way. He approaches the game the right way. I've seen way too many times, a lot of guys come to the league, and they think they know it all. He came in the league, and immediately he was ready to be a sponge around all the veterans. He listened. He paid attention. He watched how other people worked. I guess that has a lot to do with [Alabama coach Nick] Saban, too, because Saban has that type of effect on that. But Jalen came into the league with a great understanding of how to already be a pro. And then he got an even better understanding of how to be a pro. That type of mindset has elevated him so much as a young guy."

Defensive end Brandon Graham

"You can tell he feels good that people believe in him because he's been consistent this entire time. But now, you can really tell that he's locked in because he's got the keys now. He's trying to make sure he takes good care of the keys. There were a lot of doubters and a lot of stuff that he had to overcome. I'm sure he's always going to keep that chip on his shoulder. That's what I appreciate the most about him. Because he's playing with a chip on his shoulder and not being overly cool about it. When people have success, people can be overly confident or walking around with too much swagger on their chest. But he's done such a great job at handling all the success that's come his way.

"His pregame speeches, everything comes from the heart. I know it comes from his heart. It just seems every word comes so easy for him. He always makes sure his message is relevant to what we're going through as a team. That's what you appreciate the most."

Kicker Jake Elliott

"It's one of those things where his leadership has always been there, so it's hard to say that it's really grown. He's gotten more comfortable with the reps that he's gotten. He's really comfortable with who he is. He's always been one of those natural leaders. He's one of those guys that when he talks, people are going to listen. He goes about his personal business in private, but he's a guy that we're going to follow because he leads by example. He's always got the right things to say, so he's an easy guy to follow.

"He's definitely the leader of this team. He goes out of his way after every game and thanks all of his teammates. He comes up to you personally, and that means something. I'm sure it means a lot to him. Just being the leader that he is, I know all the guys really appreciate it. Coming from him, knowing that you put in just a little part, it's really cool to see." ■

Jalen Hurts' teammates speak glowingly about his stoic, determined, and direct approach to leading the team. (David Maialetti / Staff Photographer)

Doing the Work

From SoCal to his locker stall — tales of an unrelenting work ethic

January 19, 2023 | By Jeff McLane

Jalen Hurts knows a hard worker when he sees one.

Tony Santiago is the Eagles' locker room custodian. He has worked 12 hours a day, six days a week — seven during training camp — for the last 19 years at the NovaCare Complex. But he has toiled in relative obscurity until Hurts name-checked him two weeks ago following the season finale.

Santiago's phone buzzed almost immediately after the All-Pro quarterback, whose locker stall he cleans daily, mentioned him by his first name when he was asked what it would take for the Eagles to win the Super Bowl.

"First, I got a text from my family saying, 'Yo, is that you? He's talking about you!'" Santiago said Wednesday. "And then my friend calls me, he asks me, 'Yo, he gave you a shout-out. Is that you?' I was like, 'I guess.'

"I didn't think there was anything behind it. I was just thinking he was giving me props."

Hurts was doing just that, he later explained, but he said he was also acknowledging a kindred worker.

"I wanted to recognize him," he said. "I talk to him. I talk to everybody. But he just comes in here and he doesn't say nothing, just does his job, and then goes. I appreciate him."

When Santiago clocks in at 6:30 a.m., Hurts often isn't far behind. When he clocks out half the day later, the quarterback is sometimes still hours away from heading home. The janitor said he mostly keeps his head down, but can't help but notice how the quarterback comports himself.

"I try not to get too into it because everybody is so busy. Jalen's a real nice guy. Real cool. ... But he's business," said Santiago, who lives in the Northeast section of Philadelphia. "He walks in and does his thing and then he goes back out and disappears and then comes back again."

The stories about Hurts' work ethic are endless, but the why behind his drive isn't as easy to pin down. It seems most NFL quarterbacks are wired similarly. The best among them are competitive freaks of nature.

But the 24-year-old's motivation is also very much his own.

"I think everybody's motivation for doing this is different, and Jalen's no different," Eagles quarterbacks coach Brian Johnson said. "He's

Jalen Hurts' formidable work ethic and progressive mindset fueled the Eagles' dominant 2022 season. (Monica Herndon / Staff Photographer)

uniquely motivated to be the best that he can be. The biggest thing for him is he understands opportunity and what's at stake."

The stakes are currently at their highest. Hurts missed two regular-season games because of a right shoulder sprain and played through pain in the finale that secured a first-round bye. When Nick Sirianni gave the team the day off after the Week 18 victory, Hurts refused and guilted the coach and some of his offensive assistants into coming in to watch film that Monday.

"I think Ms. Sirianni gave me a hard time about that one. And his kids," Hurts said. "I told her we have business to attend to."

Hurts has been holding back assistants from seeing their families dating back to his high school years at Channelview outside Houston. His coach was his father, Averion, and he demanded much of his son. He was also a product of his environment in college, having played for the onerous Nick Saban at Alabama.

But Hurts' diligence, many close to him have said, is mostly innate. He has interests outside football, like music and food, but his schedule often keeps him occupied, especially in-season.

"He's a grinder. ... He doesn't leave the building; whether it's 9 at night, 10 at night, he's here. He doesn't stop," Eagles offensive coordinator Shane Steichen said. "I think when you're obsessed with your craft, you're going to be really good at what you do."

But is there a danger in being too obsessed?

"The only question people might ask is, 'Is he going to burn himself out? Is he having fun with it?'" Eagles reserve quarterback Ian Book said. "But that's just his personality. He's been doing this his whole life, acting like this. This is who he is."

It's hard to argue with the results, especially over the last year. Last offseason, the Eagles actually explored the possibility of trading for Russell Wilson or Deshaun Watson. But surely they're glad they didn't, as Hurts delivered an MVP-worthy third season.

When the season ends, the Eagles are likely to engage in contract extension negotiations with their quarterback. The front office will ask difficult questions about his ultimate worth, most of them directed to his on-field performance.

But there's also the unknown in how he will handle the potential distractions that come with age and money. Jason Kelce, for one, said the Eagles have nothing to worry about.

"Everything he wants to do is not motivated by money, is not motivated by fame, is not motivated by any outside source other than him just wanting to be the best in the world," the veteran Eagles center said. "And the guys that end up being the best in the world very intrinsically want to be the best in the world and they have a competitiveness and a desire to make that happen."

A progressive mindset

Hurts' weekly process begins almost immediately after games. He's jubilant following victories, of course. The captain took over the role of breaking the team down following Sirianni's postgame messages this season, and while he has routinely harped on "left money on the table," his parting missive to enjoy the wins is Hurts at his most exultant.

Jalen Hurts celebrates on the field following the Eagles' NFC championship win against the 49ers at Lincoln Financial Field. (Monica Herndon / Staff Photographer)

But the moment doesn't normally last long. On flights home, while most players are celebrating or mingling in the back, Hurts will walk up to first class, iPad in hand, ready to review the film with Johnson and the other offensive coaches.

"I've seen him walk by me. I didn't know that's what he was doing up there, but I'm not surprised," Book said. "He tells me that after games he has a lot on his mind that he wants to watch right after."

If the Eagles are home, and they start in the afternoon, Johnson's phone will ring later that evening sometime around 10 or 10:30 p.m. while he's watching Sunday Night Football.

"And my wife's like, 'Who's that?'" Johnson said. "'It's Jalen.'"

They'll FaceTime and go over plays and successful decision-making, but Hurts wants to focus more on his errors. He said he can't move on until he has evaluated what he did wrong and learned how to improve upon it.

"It's in my mind, I guess," he said. "To me, I always want to be in a progressive mindset of, 'How can I make progress? How can I learn from mistakes? How can I learn from what I just did that will help me be better the next time around?'"

On Mondays, there is a formal review with corrections at NovaCare. The entire team is in attendance, but while most players head home afterward, Hurts often sticks around. He'll receive treatment or get a workout in.

Hurts has a setup at home that allows him to study film on a screen larger than his iPad, Book said. But on Tuesdays, the players' day off, he's back at the team facility and by the evening ready to digest the game plan for the next opponent that coaches spent the day devising.

"He's the one in here till all hours of the night," Sirianni said. "He's the one in here popping his head in the Tuesday night offensive coaches meeting and seeing if Brian Johnson is still in there so he can continue to go over the game plan when it's 9 o'clock at night."

It isn't atypical for quarterbacks to come in on days off, or to get a jump on game plans, or stay later than other players. But it is uncommon to see one on the VersaClimber in the weight room, with midnight approaching, as Johnson described seeing Hurts one random Tuesday as he departed the building.

Hurts' father raised him to powerlift, and tales of his prodigious strength stretch back years. Kelce saw it firsthand while training alongside him at Eagles tackle Lane Johnson's "Bro Barn" in Moorestown during the 2021 offseason.

But the center said Hurts has broken away from maxing out on lifts.

"Most quarterbacks aren't workout warriors in the weight room," Kelce said. "They're different types of athletes. Sometimes I questioned it like, 'Is it necessary for you to squat or deadlift what I'm doing?' But I think in a lot of ways he's grown away from that, as well."

The instinctual ability

Hurts, coming off his first year with Sirianni's staff, approached the 2022 offseason differently. Some of the suggestions came from the Eagles. Brian Johnson said Hurts was given a detailed plan on areas in which he needed to improve, with his timing — "finding your

Jalen Hurts celebrates with center Jason Kelce after throwing a touchdown pass during a September win over the Washington Commanders. (David Maialetti / Staff Photographer)

rhythm of understanding when the ball's supposed to be out," he said — at the top of the list.

There are myriad variables in how to achieve that. In March, Hurts went to 3DQB, the elite passing academy in Huntington Beach, Calif., where NFL quarterbacks from Tom Brady to Lamar Jackson have worked on their throwing mechanics.

Carson Wentz first went there in 2017 following his rookie season with the Eagles. Some NFL coaches have trepidation about outside gurus turning their quarterbacks into robots, but 3DQB CEO Adam Dedeaux and his instructors are renowned and Johnson said Hurts needed repetitions to fine-tune the sequencing of his throwing motion.

Before heading out, he hit up Dallas Goedert, who has worked out at 3DQB every offseason. The Eagles tight end said that he caught passes from Hurts every Monday, Tuesday, and Thursday for about a month and that he got to see up close how a few tweaks improved his passing.

"The first couple throws — it felt different for him. So the throws weren't perfect," Goedert said. "Sometimes he would throw the 'out' and his shoulder would be here and it would be a little bit high. They wanted him to get that shoulder down so he could have more zip, more velocity, and be on a line.

"And he's like, 'OK, I feel what you're saying.'"

Goedert said Hurts would have him run the same routes over and over as he worked on the various drops he may throw from, but more so the many different platforms and arm angles when he's forced to improvise.

He said that he observed how Hurts was often at his best when left to his own devices — almost as if he were playing backyard football — and that he increasingly didn't want tips during drills, only after.

Hurts may be disciplined, but he isn't regimented by outside voices, Kelce said. In the veteran's opinion, the players who follow only the advice of others when it comes to eating, sleeping, lifting, etc. are often the ones who fail on the football field.

And the best quarterbacks follow their inner compass, he said, more than anything or anyone else.

"The beauty of his game, or Patrick Mahomes or Peyton Manning and Tom Brady — they aren't robots," Kelce said. "They can operate in this regimented mode, but they also have the instinctual ability to then make things happen that aren't designed or concrete.

"Nobody's going to be the best player in the world by listening to a bunch of people telling them what to do. You take that information and you make it whatever it is that works for you. Jalen puts in hard work, but he's also creative and instinctual."

But there's plenty to be said for grinding. Once Hurts returned from Southern California, he organized passing days with various receivers. And when Eagles spring workouts ended in June, Goedert, receiver A.J. Brown, and several others met him in Miami for a players-only camp.

Hurts' throwing workouts sometimes took place at odd hours. Backup quarterback Gardner Minshew lived in an old prison bus during the offseason and during OTAs the Eagles allowed him to park it at NovaCare.

"One night I was sneaking into the building to get a little snack at about 8 o'clock and freaking Jalen was in the indoor [bubble] throwing to somebody, you know, with the lights on," Minshew said. "That guy is just committed to just getting better. It's never an ego."

On a mission

Hurts' stall is tucked in the corner at the front of the Eagles' locker room — the traditional spot for starting quarterbacks. Santiago has seen them all come and go — from Donovan McNabb to Michael

Vick, from Nick Foles to Hurts, who he said keeps his space tidy.

"He's pretty good at keeping it because that's his mentality," Santiago said.

Amid the usual clutter of Hurts' shoes, clothes, and equipment are some personal touches. There's a scarf from his fraternity, Omega Psi Phi, hanging from a hook. A couple of small decals — "'Bama A Club" and "Women In Sports Social Club" — are stuck on one side. Taped to the back of the stall are letters and artwork from young fans.

But on one shelf is the centerpiece, a plate with Michael Jordan's image and his quote: "Some people want it to happen, some wish it would happen, and others MAKE IT happen."

Hurts may wander into the locker room at times during the three 45-minute periods allotted to reporters during the week. He's normally either getting suited up for practice or breaking down afterward, but there have been a few occasions when he seems to be relaxing.

His speaker might be playing some slow jam, like Mint Condition's "Breakin' My Heart (Pretty Brown Eyes)" and he'll welcome a question or two. Hurts' musical tastes run the gamut, but his old-school leanings reflect what many close to him describe as an "old soul."

He doesn't frequent clubs, casinos or parties, his friends on the Eagles said.

"For him to be social, somebody got to cook," Eagles receiver Quez Watkins said. "Usually it's him and his crawfish. But somebody else might have a barbecue. And then we might go bowling, or do something simple like that."

Crawfish boils are serious business in the Hurts family. During the offseason, Jalen walked Eagles executive chef James Sirles through his process. He has other outside interests aside from music and food, fashion being one.

Hurts gifted Eagles offensive linemen Louis Vuitton travel bags and his fellow quarterbacks vintage Air Jordan 11s for Christmas. His game-day attire is often flashy, but his friends on the team said he's just as comfortable in sweatsuits away from the spotlight.

Some teammates don't get to see that side of Hurts away from the facility. Book said Hurts may banter with the quarterbacks about a subject outside of football "once or twice a week" for "about 10 minutes," but he stops talking long before the others.

"If you didn't know him you would be like, 'Man, is he serious all the time? Does he ever have fun? Does he ever smile?'" Book said. "And then you realize that he just wants to be great. A lot of people say that, but you can tell he's on a mission. ... He's not ready to smile yet. He's ready to become the best and then smile."

Hurts may be worth $200 million by the time he turns 25 on Aug. 7. Those around him said they don't believe he'll be distracted the more complicated his life becomes as the face of a franchise.

Hurts doesn't seem to be looking that far ahead. He doesn't have much interest in probing questions about his innermost motivations. Asked if he thinks much about the sacrifices he has made in his social life or otherwise, he shook his head.

"Because I know what I desire," Hurts said. "I know what I want. I know what my goals and my dreams are. And I just try to put forth the effort to do those things every day."

Workers work. Santiago knows. He said he doesn't mind when the players get messy.

"They'll be apologetic about it. But, hey, those guys are busy," Santiago said. "They're doing their jobs. I just try to keep up." ∎

Breed of One

Jalen Hurts is the Eagles' answer to Michael Jordan. Just ask them. And him.

January 22, 2023 | By Mike Sielski

The heavy, silver, spangled chain that encircled Jalen Hurts' neck late Saturday night would have made Mr. T jealous and sent Lil Wayne to a jeweler with a special request to help him keep pace in the arms race of bling. Dangling from the necklace's center like a talisman was a fist-sized plate of sparkling stones that spelled out three words: BREED OF ONE. It was no wonder Hurts wore it. He thinks himself that. To listen to the Eagles talk about him in the aftermath of their 38-7 thrashing of the Giants, with the NFC championship game a week away, was to get the sense that they think of him that way, too.

"I know this is high praise, but to have him out there is like having — I'm not sure I should go there — Michael Jordan out there," coach Nick Sirianni said. "He's your leader. He's your guy. Hopefully, that's the biggest respect I can pay to him, comparing his ability to be on the field to a Michael Jordan-type thing. This guy leads. He brings this calmness to the entire team. He plays great football. He's tough as they come. To me, there's nobody playing any better football than him."

They might have a case out in Kansas City, where Patrick Mahomes suffered what appeared to be a serious ankle injury Saturday afternoon against the Jaguars — so severe that Mahomes could hardly set his foot on the ground without wincing and limping — and still led the Chiefs to a 27-20 win. Hurts, though, took the Eagles to a different place merely through his presence and his return to full health.

His numbers were relatively modest: 154 passing yards, 34 rushing yards, a third-quarter sack/fumble. But he threw two touchdown passes and ran for another, and the most revealing aspect of how he performed Saturday was that it was no different from how he had performed before spraining his shoulder last month in Chicago against the Bears. Sirianni and offensive coordinator Shane Steichen placed no restrictions on Hurts in their play-calling, and Hurts placed none on himself in carrying out those calls.

"We were going to run the best things that were best for us, knowing that Jalen [had] no limitations," Sirianni said. "If that was running him, that was running him. We don't think, 'Hey, we're going to show you guys.' He was ready to go with what he did.

Jalen Hurts runs with the football while wearing Air Jordan XI cleats. He garnered Michael Jordan comparisons from his head coach following the 38-7 thrashing of the rival Giants in the divisional round. (David Maialetti / Staff Photographer)

Again, that doesn't mean he's always going to carry it, because some of that is determined by the defense. But when he does carry it, he demands that respect on the backside. Nothing was off limits tonight."

On the Eagles' second play from scrimmage, Hurts lofted a perfect deep ball to DeVonta Smith for 40 yards. In the fourth quarter, on third-and-2, he cut away from Giants linebacker Kayvon Thibodeaux and lunged forward for 4 yards and a first down, not turning away from contact but inviting it. The injury, by all indications, inhibited neither his ability to throw or his willingness to run — to be the quarterback he has been all season, which is just about the best quarterback in the NFL. And it restored the sharpness and explosiveness that the Eagles offense had been missing in those final two regular-season games. Two drives to start Saturday for the Eagles, two touchdowns, in large part because the Giants had no idea what the Eagles would do from snap to snap, because with Hurts in there, they can do just about anything.

"It makes things so much easier for us," center Jason Kelce said. "He's a legitimate threat to run, and we try to limit it so we're not making him prone to injury. But when he can scramble and he's healthy, that makes it harder to rush the passer. That makes it harder to defend the run. It's another element that puts the numbers in our favor. He was definitely making it very easy early on with some of the things he was doing."

How much Hurts still hurts remains a mystery. When he was asked after the game how his shoulder felt, he said: "Good enough. ... Regardless of how I was feeling physically, mentally I was already there. There was nothing that needed to be done for me to get there."

He seems to relish the idea that he is withstanding a significant measure of pain, as if it enhances his standing in his teammates' eyes, his coaches' eyes, and in his own. Sirianni hesitated before dropping that Jordan comparison, and there's no doubt that Hurts isn't completely healthy. But Jordan was a master at motivating himself by building obstacles to be overcome and turning an opponent's innocuous quotes into egregious slights, and Hurts seems wired in the same manner — and has been since his arrival here. After missing two games, he donned a Jordan-themed "I'M BACK" T-shirt for the Eagles' regular-season finale. And remember: Carson Wentz didn't just lose the team's starting quarterback job. Hurts made it clear to the entire organization, once he entered the lineup late in the 2020 season, that he wasn't about to give it back.

"The first day he stepped in at Green Bay, I felt like he was dialed in," tight end Dallas Goedert said. "I don't know what everybody else was looking at, but he's been a dog since he got here — I can tell you that."

A dog. A breed of one. A cut above every other quarterback in the NFL. That's Jalen Hurts in his own mind. That's more and more a reality difficult to deny. If he and the Eagles win twice more, who could argue with him? ∎

Injuries may have limited Jalen Hurts against the Giants, but he did more than enough to help the Eagles clinch a spot in the NFC championship. (David Maialetti / Staff Photographer)

From Unwanted to NFC Champion

Jalen Hurts arrived in Philadelphia as a curiosity. Less than three years later, he's Super Bowl-bound.

January 29, 2023 | By Matt Breen

Jalen Hurts, pairing a lavender jacket with lavender pants, sat alone Sunday night at his locker in the corner of the Eagles locker room and puffed a cigar. His work — a year after his season ended with criticism and uncertainty — was finished. The Eagles are NFC champions. And Hurts had the smoke to prove it.

He had arrived in Philadelphia as a curiosity, a backup quarterback selected in the second round who was first used as a gadget player. He even said after Sunday's 31-7 win over the 49ers that "they probably didn't even want to draft me here."

Less than three years later, he's the fourth player to quarterback the Eagles to the Super Bowl. He completed 15 of his 25 passes, rushed for a game-sealing score in the final minute of the third quarter, and did not record a turnover.

Hurts' banner season — he was the MVP favorite before a shoulder injury sidelined him for two of the final three regular-season games — will finish in the Super Bowl. That may have seemed lofty a year ago when Hurts and the Eagles were easily bounced in the opening round by Tampa Bay. What a difference a year made.

"It was a big surprise to many," Hurts said when asked to clarify his comments about people not wanting to draft him. "But my favorite [Bible] verse — I went through a lot of stuff in college and it kind of stuck with me — is John 13:7. 'You may not know now but later you'll understand.' Hopefully, people understand."

Hurts lost his starting job at Alabama at halftime of the 2018 national championship game and spent a year as a backup before transferring to Oklahoma. Pundits were skeptical if he had the arm and pocket presence to quarterback in the NFL. He's done his best to silence that this season.

"I have a lot of respect for guys who battle," tackle Lane Johnson said. "That's what football is about. It's about battling and facing adversity and going through it."

Hurts has completed 58% of his passes in two playoff wins, rushing for a score in each blowout victory. He is playing this postseason with a sore

Jalen Hurts gets a hug from team owner Jeff Lurie after the Eagles' win in the NFC championship game over the San Francisco 49ers. (David Maialetti / Staff Photographer)

shoulder but did not appear limited by it Sunday, nor did he shy away from contact when rushing the ball.

He carried the Eagles for the first 14 weeks of the season and is proving to be the type of QB — one who makes plays without making mistakes — who wins in the postseason. The QBs the Eagles have faced in the playoffs — the Giants' Daniel Jones and the 49ers' Brock Purdy and Josh Johnson — combined for three turnovers. The difference in QB play has been stark.

"I know I've been through a lot personally, but I don't want to steer away from the direction of how good this team has been at playing together, being together, and challenging one another," Hurts said. "When we experienced some painful times and some tough times, we always found a way to overcome. You want to be going into a situation like this, and we have a chance to go out there and win it all, so we want to prepare to go do that."

The game only felt tenuous for a few minutes after Christian McCaffrey tied the score at 7 by leaping over and barreling through a cast of Eagles defenders. Hurts answered back, orchestrating a 14-play drive that lasted nearly seven minutes and ended with a Miles Sanders TD run. The rout was on.

"We found a way to get it going," Hurts said. "It looked different, and that's been the thing with this whole entire team and this whole entire offense this year. We come out there and throw for a lot. We go out there and run for a lot. We come out there and we're just kind of efficient."

How important is Hurts to the Eagles? They flew Anita Baker — the Grammy-winning soul singer whom Hurts frequently mentions as one of his favorite artists — to sing the national anthem. Soon, they could match that affection with a contract extension. The questions that once hovered around Hurts have seemed to dissipate like a cloud of smoke

"All I know and this is a fact — he's about to get paid," Jordan Mailata said. "Oh my God. Oh my God. Pay the man."

Jalen Hurts celebrates the gratifying NFC championship win with teammates. (Yong Kim / Staff Photographer)

The man who would pay that extension — Eagles owner Jeffrey Lurie — called Hurts a "great young leader" and "terrific quarterback."

"When we drafted him, it was the upside we were banking on," Lurie said. "We thought he had a huge upside. It takes a couple years. Someone who is so dedicated as Jalen and such a great teammate, inevitably he's going to maximize everything he has. That's what he's done."

Hurts' development this season to be considered a franchise QB is often credited to a tireless work ethic, something Mailata sees every night at the team's practice complex.

"Sometimes I stay back just to do recovery and he stays back to watch the film with the coach," Mailata said. "I joke around and say, 'I'm going to try and beat you, man. I'm going to stay here the longest.' He's like, 'Yeah, but you're doing nothing.' I was like, 'Damn.' We get in at 7:30, get done at 5:30, and he's still there watching film until 7:30. I'll try to get one on him."

It didn't take long Sunday for the stage to be constructed on the field after the clock struck zero. Hurts soon stood on top, waiting to hold the NFC championship trophy as confetti littered the field. He pulled off his jersey and shoulder pads, swapping them for a championship hat and shirt.

Once an uncertainty, Hurts held a microphone and led the raucous crowd in the team's fight song. The Eagles, thanks to the QB who silenced the critics, were again Super Bowl-bound. The only thing left to do was light one up.

"It's not a time for reflection," Hurts said. "It's really hard for me to do that. I try to enjoy the moment, but my joy comes from winning. I know the job isn't done. I never knew how far we'd go, but I never said it couldn't be done." ■

While he may have been overlooked during his early NFL days, Jalen Hurts made his superstar presence known to the league in leading the Eagles to Super Bowl LVII. (David Maialetti / Staff Photographer)

'You Either Win or You Learn'

Jalen Hurts went toe-to-toe with Patrick Mahomes. A fumble short in the Super Bowl, he shouldn't have 'any doubters left.'

February 13, 2023 | By Jeff McLane

Jalen Hurts stood face-to-face with Patrick Mahomes after they went toe-to-toe in Super Bowl LVII.

Hurts had already showered and changed and was heading to his postgame interview in one of the tunnels under State Farm Stadium. Mahomes was still in uniform with a championship hat worn backward on his head and a few strands of confetti at his feet.

"Hell of a game," Mahomes said as they embraced. "Hell of a game."

The Chiefs quarterback's comment was in reference to Hurts' performance in his first NFL title game. But he just as easily could have been talking about the shootout between two explosive offenses in which the Eagles quarterback nearly matched the league's MVP.

Mahomes, though, had the final say — at least until eight seconds were left — when kicker Harrison Butker's 27-yard field goal capped a second-half rally and squeaked Kansas City past the Eagles, 38-35, on Sunday night.

If Mahomes, in his second MVP-winning Super Bowl victory, outplayed his counterpart, it was by the smallest of margins. But he had no turnovers and Hurts did — a second-quarter fumble that was returned for a touchdown — and that was a costly mistake.

"Obviously, I try and control the things that I can, not just the ball every play, so I just try and protect it," Hurts said. "But, it hurt us."

It wasn't by any stretch the lone error the Eagles made, especially by their defense and punt cover unit in the second half. And Hurts was resilient, driving the offense to another touchdown on the ensuing drive and playing high-level football for the remainder of the evening.

He completed 27 of 38 passes for 304 yards and a touchdown. He rushed 15 times for a Super Bowl quarterback-record 70 yards and three touchdowns. And when the Eagles needed a two-point conversion to knot the score at 35 with just over five minutes remaining, he ran power left and lunged himself — despite a still-tender shoulder — over the goal line.

Despite Jalen Hurts playing what Eagles coach Nick Sirianni called "the best game I've seen him play," the Eagles fell to the Chiefs in Super Bowl LVII. (Monica Herndon / Staff Photographer)

"Jalen played the best game I've seen him play," Eagles coach Nick Sirianni said, "in the two years that we've been together."

The numbers don't do Hurts' outing justice. He was accurate with his arm in the tense moments — two third-down tight-window tosses to tight end Dallas Goedert stood out — fleet of foot when the Eagles needed him on the ground, and never seemed out of his element in the biggest game of his career.

"If there were any doubters left there shouldn't be now," Mahomes said. "I mean, the way he stepped on this stage, and ran, threw the ball, whatever it took for his team to win. I mean, that was a special performance. I don't want it to get lost in the loss that they had."

The 24-year-old Hurts came within a whisker of becoming the first true dual threat to win a Super Bowl. Running quarterbacks have won before — see: Steve Young and Russell Wilson — but never one who was a plus-one factor in the run game.

The myth that those types of quarterbacks can't thrive in the NFL had long been dispelled, but so was the notion that Hurts was a "system quarterback" who couldn't carry an offense with his arm — long before Sunday's game.

And yet, Cowboys linebacker Micah Parsons and 49ers kicker Robbie Gould, among others, continued to question his quarterbacking aptitude this season.

"I said I was proud of him," said tackle Jordan Mailata, who put his arm on Hurts after his last fateful pass fell to the turf. "Everything he's accomplished this year, everything he's overcome — all the branding, things that people have been saying in the media. The guy threw for 300 yards, [rushed for] three touchdowns.

"Not bad for a system QB, right?"

Philadelphia Eagles quarterback Jalen Hurts gets a two point conversion to tie the score 35-35 in the fourth quarter of Super Bowl LVII against the Kansas City Chiefs at State Farm Stadium on Sunday, Feb. 12, 2023, in Glendale, AZ.

There's no denying that Hurts as a threat in the zone read, run-pass-run option game played a role in the Eagles' offensive success once Sirianni decided midseason a year ago to cater the scheme to his mobility. It opened lanes for the running backs and kept defenses guessing.

It's clearly sustainable, but once Hurts signs a contract extension, he's no longer a quarterback playing on a second-round rookie deal. He's the franchise and the Eagles will need to protect their investment. The shoulder injury he suffered on a designed run in Chicago shouldn't be forgotten.

A deal somewhere in the $50 million-a-year department will also force general manager Howie Roseman to make some tough decisions with 20 pending free agents this offseason.

"It's going to be interesting to see what happens," said center Jason Kelce, who said he will take some time before deciding if he will retire. "Obviously, the team is going to look pretty different next year. But I think the future is very bright for Jalen."

There will also be change in the coaching staff. Offensive coordinator Shane Steichen is reportedly slated to become the Colts' next head coach, and defensive coordinator Jonathan Gannon will interview for the Cardinals' opening this week.

Quarterbacks coach Brian Johnson is the likely

Jalen Hurts scores a touchdown in the second quarter of Super Bowl LVII. Hurts rushed 15 times for a Super Bowl quarterback-record 70 yards and three touchdowns against the Chiefs. (Heather Khalifa / Staff Photographer)

in-house replacement for Steichen. So Sirianni has some stability on his staff.

But the one constant will be the unflappable Hurts. He publicly handled the disappointment of the loss like a pro. He's been down this road before, of course, having fallen short in the college national championship as a freshman, and then getting benched the following year when Alabama rebounded to win.

"You either win or you learn," Hurts said when asked to describe his emotion on Sunday, "that's how I feel."

He's known for his stoic demeanor, his "Jalen face," which became a meme for how the coach's son doesn't alter his guise — win, lose or draw. But a few Eagles staffers referenced Hurts' emotion in the locker room afterward when he apologized to the team for his fumble.

"I don't do this to be loved. I don't do this to be hated," Hurts said when asked about the apology. "I don't do this to seek anyone else's approval. I do it for the guys in the locker room."

Earlier, once the Eagles' locker room opened, Hurts was initially absent. But he eventually showed up. And as cornerback James Bradberry took blame for his late-game holding penalty, as Kelce pulled confetti from his cleats after congratulating his brother, Travis, and as Eagles players, coaches, and staffers comforted each other, Hurts stood at his locker stall and ate a peanut butter and jelly sandwich.

Eagles owner Jeffrey Lurie and his son, Julian, looked on.

"Awesome," Lurie said of Hurts' performance. "Can't wait till next season with this guy. He's special."

Hurts eventually was escorted to the interview area and had to walk by the celebratory Chiefs' locker room. Andy Reid's wife, Tammy, hugged him. Linebacker Carlos Dunlap, offensive coordinator Eric Bieniemy, and Mahomes offered words of encouragement.

"I know he's hurt," Sirianni said, "and he's hurting."

On the surface he was the same emotionless Hurts. He chose his words carefully during his nine-minute news conference in which he fielded 13 questions. The last, from 14-year-old Giovanni Hamilton, an Eagles superfan who has Schwartz-Jampel syndrome, asked Hurts if there was a lesson to be learned for next season.

"Obviously, we had a big-time goal that we wanted to accomplish, and we came up short," Hurts said. "I think the beautiful part about it is everyone experiences different pains, everyone experiences different agonies of life, but you decide if you want to learn from it.

"You decide if you want that to be a teachable moment. I know I do."

Hurts then walked out of the room, grabbed his belongings and walked toward the exit with Mailata. When he reached the buses, he made a detour toward A.J. Brown and DeVonta Smith, who were sitting on a golf cart waiting until the last second to board.

The quarterback shook each wide receiver's hand, picked up his bag, and at 9:41 p.m. Mountain Time ascended the steps and departed for the team hotel, his future unwritten, but seemingly destined to return to this Super spectacle. ∎

When asked how he felt after the Eagles' loss to the Chiefs, Jalen Hurts responded, "You either win or you learn." (Monica Herndon / Staff Photographer)

The Last Word

From Reading Terminal Market to the site of a Jalen Hurts mural in Fairmount, Birds fans want star quarterback Jalen Hurts to know they're grateful for the great season

February 14, 2023 | By Ximena Conde

After the Philadelphia Eagles lost to Kansas City Sunday, star quarterback Jalen Hurts apologized to his teammates for his fumble in the first half.

"You either win or you learn," with the emphasis on the "learn," was Hurts' refrain to reporters.

Known for being stoic, Hurts appeared deflated, bordering contrite, in the moments after a heartbreaking loss on a national stage. Birds fans mirrored his demeanor that night and in the days to follow.

Still, the fans had a refrain of their own for their team, especially their quarterback: thank you.

The day after the Super Bowl loss, Bill Strobel encouraged people to come to the Fairmount section of the city, where he'd painted a Hurts mural, and show their support. By Tuesday, the mural of Hurts in action, ready to throw the ball an unspecified number of yards, was covered with chalk messages echoing the sentiment.

"You inspire us," read the bottom right corner with "MVP" scrawled right on top.

"Hurts + Eagles forever," read another message.

If there was any anger or frustration among Philadelphia fans after the loss, it was directed at officials

In between sips of his Corona on Monday at Max's Eagle Bar, 35-year-old Elon Jackson joked the penalty that cost his team the game was an "inside job by the NFL scriptwriters."

At Reading Terminal Market, Reuben Austin, 62, tried to move past his indignation by rocking his Eagles hat as a way to signal the season was a successful one regardless of the outcome.

"We're proud of what they did and we know they'll be back because they're a team on the way up," said Austin, between lunch bites. "I don't think we've seen the best of them yet."

For Austin and others, much of their hope remains nested in Hurts, whom they were hard pressed to criticize after what they described as a blockbuster performance. Fans fired off stats. Hurts threw for 304 yards and a touchdown, running for 70 yards and three touchdowns, they clamored. How could they be upset with him?

As if to ensure Hurts heard their message, fans continued to flood social media with messages of support.

Muralist Bill Stroebel paints a mural of Jalen Hurts at Brown and Corinthian in the Fairmount section of Philadelphia. (Alejandro A. Alvarez / Staff Photographer)

One user took to Twitter on Tuesday to talk about how Hurts had inspired them.

"If you were ever looked over or had people doubt that you would ever be anything in life, you get it," read the post saying thanks. "Once you know what failure feels like, you look at losses differently."

Hurts' struggles in his final collegiate years, when he was demoted as backup quarterback in Alabama before transferring to Oklahoma, are no secret. Even in the Birds' Cinderella season, Hurts faced criticism from doubters like analyst Chris Simms — who later admitted he was wrong.

And Hurts has been open about how his arrival to Philly must have been a surprise to many.

"They probably didn't even want to draft me here," he said in a news conference after beating the 49ers in the NFC championship game.

If that was once true, Hurts should have no doubt he is now synonymous with the team, known for his work ethic.

"We came out of last year not seeing this at all," said Strobel, who painted the Fairmount mural — one of at least two Hurts murals that sprung up around the city ahead of the Super Bowl.

"It was like he was still on a 'prove it to me' kind of a situation," Strobel said, "and he came out and all he did was just be one of the top quarterbacks in the whole league and his record was amazing as a starter and he says all the right things."

Strobel had a note of his own against the black backdrop of his mural, though he kept it simple:

"Thank you." ■

Eagles fan Charles Allen writes a "thank you" message to Jalen Hurts on Feb. 14, 2023. Following the Eagles' Super Bowl loss, artist Bill Strobel encouraged people to come out to Fairmount, where he'd painted a mural of Hurts, to show their support. Within two days, the mural was covered with chalk messages.

THE
LEGACY

Embracing the Legacy

With Jalen Hurts, the Eagles build on a history of Black QBs in Philadelphia

September 8, 2022 | By Jeff McLane

Jalen Hurts knows his history. He knows his Eagles history.

He knows of the long, bleak past when African American men who had as much ability to play quarterback as any white man were denied that opportunity by the NFL. He knows about the pioneers who in cracking that door open endured overt racism.

Hurts also knows about the next generation of Black quarterbacks who faced some of the same challenges and yet persevered. He knows that the Eagles organization was in many ways ground zero for that rise — from Randall Cunningham to Donovan McNabb and Michael Vick — and how each inspired countless young men to pursue the same dream.

He knows because growing up in Houston, he wanted to be one of them.

And now as the latest manifestation, he is one of them.

"When I got drafted to Philly, it felt like, I don't know, destiny," Hurts said when asked about following in the footsteps of Cunningham, McNabb, and Vick. "I've definitely modeled my game in different ways around all of them over the years as I've grown and as I kind of hold this torch up of being the next dual-threat African American quarterback in Philly and knowing what that means to them and to this franchise.

"It's important to me."

No other franchise in NFL history has as many starts from Black quarterbacks as the Eagles. Their prominent place in that hierarchy may be circumstance, or may not be, but either way, it's a legacy the 24-year-old embraces.

Hurts, who said he has relationships with Cunningham, McNabb, and Vick, chose his words carefully when asked recently if he wants to be known as a "Black quarterback." Cunningham, nearly four decades ago, downplayed the cultural significance of his ascent to the position, even if he was still subject to the same stereotypes.

Hurts is cognizant of the once long-held belief that African Americans weren't mentally or physically equipped to handle the demands of being a quarterback and that many who had played the position in college were moved to wide receiver or defensive back.

When the name Jimmy Raye, the former Michigan State quarterback who played briefly for the Eagles, was brought up, Hurts knew that he had

Jalen Hurts proudly follows in the footsteps of previous Eagles quarterbacks Randall Cunningham, Donovan McNabb, and Michael Vick. No other NFL franchise has as many starts from Black quarterbacks as the Eagles. (David Maialetti / Staff Photographer)

been converted into a defensive back after the Rams drafted him in 1968. Sometimes those decisions are made years earlier, and he understands that dynamic still exists, and if he can have any impact on changing it, he welcomes it.

"I am a quarterback. I look at it as that," Hurts said during an interview. "But I know we live in a world where some things mean a little more. I feel like, for me, a lot of kids who come up, just because he's athletic, they want to change his position because he's not the prototype. And those are typically the Black kids.

"I was a kid where I came out and I went to the best college in the country [Alabama]. Coach [Nick] Saban didn't ask me to change my position, not once. I take pride in that. I take pride in being a quarterback. And I take pride in what it means to be an African American quarterback because I know it's not about me. I know how hard it was to get to this point.

"I know the people before me, the Warren Moons, one of the best quarterbacks to play the game, he had to go to a whole other league to prove himself. … There's a deeper meaning to it all."

When Moon, after six seasons in the Canadian Football League, finally got his chance with the Houston Oilers in 1984, only 11 African Americans had started at quarterback in the 64-year history of the NFL. This season, the same number of Black quarterbacks are projected as starters.

There are Super Bowl winners, MVPs, and perennial Pro Bowlers in that group. Patrick Mahomes, Russell Wilson, and Kyler Murray are among the highest-paid players in the history of the league and are the faces of their franchises.

"There's clearly a cultural significance to these Black men rising to this position of power in the most important position in team sports, and not just team sports," said Jason Reid, the longtime NFL writer whose book, *Rise of the Black Quarterback,* was recently published. "If we take it off the field … quarterback is a uniquely American leadership position, not only confined to football. If you look at corporate America, if you're leading a big project for a company, you're considered the quarterback of that project.

"We think of the brightest among us, we think of the best among us, we think of the person who inspires everyone around them. And if Black men are excluded from that position, as they were for most of NFL history, what does that say about Black people in America, overall?"

Despite the advancements made, just a few years ago several members of NFL scouting departments and the media argued that Lamar Jackson couldn't play quarterback in the NFL. Some believe that race played a role in keeping Colin Kaepernick out of the league after his protest against police brutality and racial inequality, and that Black quarterbacks still face additional scrutiny because they don't fit traditional norms.

There are still four teams that have had less than 2% of their starts made by a Black quarterback. The league average, according to the website readjack.com, is 11.2% since 1953. That's when Willie Thrower became the first conventional quarterback to toss passes since the ban on all African Americans was lifted seven years earlier.

It was the Bears' low number in 2019 — they've since increased their percentage with Justin Fields — that compelled Chicago sports historian Jack Silverstein to do the research and compile the full team-by-team listing.

There could be any number of reasons, most of them having nothing to do with race, why some teams have had more starts by Black quarterbacks than others. But as Silverstein discovered, it often took the success of one to persuade other teams to follow suit. It has always been a copycat league.

But there were key teams — not to mention key figures in leadership roles — in that progression. The Eagles' figure of 360 starts heading into the 2022 season is 24 more than the Oilers/Titans franchise and 126 more than the next team, the Buccaneers.

"You can't tell the story of the rise of Black quarterbacks in the NFL," Reid said, "without talking about the Philadelphia Eagles."

Cunningham was the spark. McNabb caught fire. And Vick, while his impact was greater in Atlanta when he became the first Black quarterback to be drafted No. 1 overall, burned his brightest in Philly.

All three had prodigious arm talent. But it was their mobility that initially gave them an added edge. Hurts has similar traits. When he talks to any one of them, he said, their advice is to play to his strengths and be "a true dual threat."

"I tell him, 'Just do you, bro,'" Vick said. "I look at him as Donovan. Donovan had the running intangibles. He had the throwing intangibles. He wasn't the fastest. And that's kind of Jalen. He's not the fastest, but he's mobile enough and he has the arm strength to get it to any part of the field.

"And now Jalen has a chance to take it a step further, be that franchise guy, and hopefully win a championship and start cementing his legacy in Philadelphia."

A dual threat

Hurts said he didn't always want to be a quarterback. But several factors made him the natural choice in youth football. His father, Averion, was a longtime high school coach and his older brother, Averion Jr., had already laid the groundwork at the position for the Hurts family. But mostly, it was his physical skills.

"I was a baseball guy growing up, so I had the strongest arm," Hurts said. "So it was known when I got to middle school I was going to have to play quarterback, because if I didn't, nobody would be able to get me the ball. So I played quarterback and it just kind of stuck since then."

Hurts' immediate role model was his brother, who played under his father at Channelview High just outside Houston. But he studied every quarterback he watched, and gravitated toward multifaceted types such as Steve McNair, Vince Young, Cam Newton, McNabb, and Vick.

He said he had McNabb and Vick jerseys growing up, and while Cunningham's heyday occurred before he was born, Hurts said he has gone back and watched his highlights. After the Eagles beat the New York Giants in December 2021, he came out to his postgame news conference in a vintage Cunningham uniform.

"You see Randall as ahead of his time," Hurts said. "He did stuff that hadn't been seen before."

Cunningham said he got bombarded with texts, emails, and social media posts when Hurts wore his kelly green No. 12. He said he designed a piece of clothing — he wouldn't offer the particulars — he intends to send to the current Eagles quarterback once he gets his size.

"I think he is more talented than I was," Cunningham said. "I think he has a great understanding of how to live the life of someone who really understands the position, what it takes, the dedication. And the thing I like about him most is just his character.

"I listen and I only hear him saying things out of wisdom. I don't hear him putting a lot of foolishness out there."

Cunningham famously staying upright after the Carl Banks hit and throwing a touchdown pass was the play Hurts cited as his favorite. For McNabb, he

recalled his 14-second scramble before tossing a downfield dime. But it was maybe Vick who inspired him the most.

"Everybody wanted to be like Vick growing up," Hurts said. He continued: "I liked the way he played. It was electrifying. And I can reflect on it now and say, 'I am who I am.' I'm growing, and I have grown. But I am who I am as a player.

"I'm going to instinctually do what I do as a player because that's what makes me the winner I am."

While there have been plenty of "dual-threat" white quarterbacks to succeed in the NFL, some have derisively viewed the phrase, particularly when used to counter "pro-style," as code for Black quarterbacks. But as offenses have shifted to include college tactics to accentuate mobility, the connotation has evolved.

Hurts acknowledged his forerunners in helping to change that narrative, and it's a description he welcomes. McNabb was once criticized by a prominent local Black leader when he became more of a pocket passer. And while Vick may have been "the first to play unapologetically 'Black,'" as Reid suggested, he was conflicted.

"I went through a lot in terms of what I grew up watching and what I felt like what the position should look like," Vick said. "You had Tom [Brady], you had Peyton [Manning], and they were winning. Do I continue to just do me?

"They wrote articles saying, 'This style won't last, he needs to become a pocket passer.' So now there's all this trauma in my head about how I'm supposed to play, and the game will never look like this. And I was like, 'You know what, I'm just going to do me,'

the same thing I'm telling Jalen now, another Black quarterback 20 years later."

Newton may have been the nexus point. Here was a Black quarterback seemingly unabashed about his style of play. When Hurts scored against the Panthers, Newton's old team, in Carolina last year, he paid homage by replicating his Superman celebration.

Newton, who is currently out of the NFL but still wants to play, received plenty of reproach for his flamboyance. McNabb once claimed he was the most criticized quarterback ever. Some of it had a racial component.

Asked if Black quarterbacks still face greater scrutiny, Hurts said, "I think there's levels to that, and I'll just leave it at that. ... I think as time goes on, things change."

Aside from touchdown celebrations, Hurts rarely shows emotion. He is very much a coach's son, but he also gets his diligence, some close to him have said, from his educator mother, Pamela. Saban was another influence in how to comport himself.

His teammates often describe his unflappable, stone-face demeanor. Wide receiver A.J. Brown and others have said Hurts can joke around and laugh, but when he's at work, he's all business. He rarely, if ever, slips publicly.

It comes with the position, but does Hurts add an extra layer to his already hard shell because he knows the amount of dissection his every word brings?

"I don't disagree," he said.

Hurts has spoken out on social issues. He gave a passionate address on the need to curb gun violence in June. He advocated for "Women Empowerment"

Jalen Hurts may still be in the early stages of his career, but he added to the legacy of Philadelphia quarterback excellence in historic fashion in 2022. (David Maialetti / Staff Photographer)

with his choice of footwear in the NFL's annual "My Cause, My Cleats" campaign last season, and made gender equality one of the messages of his camp for kids this summer.

At the start of his rookie season, Hurts was among a handful of Black Eagles players who raised their fists during the national anthem to protest racial inequality. Others took a knee during those last few protests.

"As I grow and mature, that will evolve," Hurts said about showing more of his personality. "But I am who I am in terms of my character, how I was raised and where it comes from. But like I said, there's levels to everything."

The breakthrough

Hurts may represent how far the Black NFL quarterback has come, and how much progress the league has made, but like many American institutions, there is an immoral history of treatment.

It was just a fledgling alliance when Fritz Pollard played for the Hammond Pros in 1923. He didn't play quarterback in the modern sense, but as the tailback in the single-wing, he is widely regarded as the first Black starting quarterback.

Joe Lillard of the Chicago Cardinals followed nine years later, but he was chased from the NFL when Boston Braves owner George Preston Marshall brokered a leaguewide ban on Black players.

The ban was lifted after 14 years in 1946, but few were given the chance to play quarterback over the next two decades. George Taliaferro threw passes as a multipurpose back, but Thrower and Charlie Brackens were the first Black quarterbacks in the modern mold to throw passes in the NFL.

It wasn't until 1968, when Marlin Briscoe was inserted for the Broncos, that an African American man was under center as the starter post-ban.

"The thought process by owners and team owners and executives and coaches was that they couldn't handle the rigors of the up-the-middle thinking man's positions, like quarterback, center, and middle linebacker, because they just weren't bright enough," Reid said. "They also weren't leaders in their estimation, and they couldn't make the calls and the adjustments."

Briscoe would be converted to a receiver the following season, however, and if there was any headway, it moved at a snail's pace over the next two decades. James Harris was the first to start and win a playoff game, in 1974. Doug Williams was the first to be drafted in the first round, in 1978.

The Eagles acquired Taliaferro late in his career, but he never threw a pass for the team. They had Raye, who was the first Black quarterback from the segregated South to win a national title, shortly after he was cut by the Rams. But he remained in the secondary and suited up for only two games before his playing career was over.

It wasn't until 1976, when new coach Dick Vermeil brought in John Walton as a backup, that the Eagles had their first bona fide Black quarterback.

"There wasn't much attention paid to it, honestly. You look back on it and it probably should have," said Ray Didinger, the Hall of Fame NFL writer who covered the team then and eventually coauthored *The Eagles Encyclopedia*. "It was pretty obvious early that he was pretty good. None of us knew very much about him coming in. Small-college guy — Elizabeth City State."

Walton threw only 65 passes over four seasons, but he threw a memorable touchdown in the Eagles' first win over the Cowboys at Texas Stadium in 1979, when he spelled the injured Ron Jaworski.

When Cunningham arrived in Philly in 1985, Williams had five seasons as a starter and Moon had made the transition from the CFL. But they were mostly pocket passers. Cunningham broke the mold with his freakish athleticism, but it took a few years before he supplanted Jaworski as the full-time starter.

"It was a tough position to be in, with Jaworski being white, but Randall handled it very well," Didinger said. "Every time someone would ask a question that had a racial component to it, Randall just sort of dismissed it and said that's not what it's all about."

Cunningham grew up in Santa Barbara, Calif. In Reid's book, he said he had never been called the N-word until he heard it on the road after a UNLV game. In Philly off the field, Cunningham was known more for his flash and mercurial personality than he was for anything pertaining to race.

"I didn't want to be distracted," Cunningham said. "It's one thing to plant seeds. But I think my best option was to do it on the field because if I didn't do anything on the field, I wouldn't be representing like I needed to. ... I didn't go through as much craziness as Doug Williams and the men of the past."

Cunningham redefined what a successful quarterback could look like in the NFL, but his failure to win in the postseason and injuries derailed his career in Philly and he eventually lost his starting spot to Rodney Peete.

Williams, meanwhile, was named Super Bowl MVP with Washington in 1987, and Peete and other Black quarterbacks began to emerge. But it was the 1999 draft, when McNabb, Akili Smith, and Daunte Culpepper were selected in the first 11 picks, that many now consider a sea change in how the position was evaluated.

It also impacted the next wave.

"I went through the process of having people that looked just like me tell me that I was going to be a receiver once I got to college," Vick said. "Told me

straight to my face and really killed my confidence. Andy [Reid], what he did in the 1999 draft taking Donovan No. 2, that did so much for me.

"That gave me so much confidence. Here's a guy that looked like me, played like me."

The talent pool was too obvious to deny. McNabb had boatloads of it and by his second season finished runner-up in MVP voting. He helped guide the Eagles to four straight NFC championship games in the early 2000s.

McNabb's relationship with Philly got off to a rocky start when fans in New York booed Andy Reid's pick — they wanted running back Ricky Williams — but the city's love for its football team and its best players is almost color-blind.

"If guys come in and perform, then that's really all the fans here are looking for," Didinger said. "And if you look at the way guys have been received here, the racial thing has never really been an issue. It really hasn't been talked about. And the only time it was talked about in a really meaningful way, in a really grab-the-headlines kind of way, it was raised by Rush Limbaugh.

"It didn't come from Philadelphia. The Black quarterback thing — that wasn't a WIP creation, that wasn't the local media, that was Rush Limbaugh. And if you remember, the city rallied behind Don."

Limbaugh, the conservative commentator who worked briefly for ESPN, downplayed McNabb's accomplishments by 2003, and said he had been overrated by a media that was "very desirous that a Black quarterback do well."

Silverstein maintained the opposite and said that a largely white media has long been complicit in the language associated with the position and that there aren't enough Black viewpoints in the field.

He made a strong case, as did Jason Reid, for both Cunningham and McNabb belonging in the Pro

Football Hall of Fame and said that traditional views on the quarterback position may have helped keep them out. It should be noted that of the 49 current Hall of Fame voters, most of whom are in the media, only seven are Black.

"I used to care, but I've kind of lost my desire now," Cunningham said about the Hall. "Back in the day it was more, 'How did that player impact his position?' And from what I've heard, I had an impact, not only on African American quarterbacks, but the style of quarterbacking.

"But I just leave it in the hands of the people. I don't want to be one of these guys who goes out there and is like, 'I'm [ticked].' I'm just grateful."

The best version

Vick wants to shine further light on the story of the Black quarterback. He said he's in the infancy stages of putting together a documentary film on the subject. He often wonders whether successful college quarterbacks from the 1990s, such as Charlie Ward or Tommie Frazier, would have gotten better opportunities in the NFL had he been around earlier.

He also wonders about the success he might have had with the Falcons had Andy Reid been his first coach or if his offensive coordinators then thought more outside the box like today's play callers.

"I just want to know more," said Vick, currently an analyst for Fox Sports. "I just wonder if the Charlie Wards would have gotten a chance. If the way I played would have been a detriment to defenses in the mid-'90s or the way they're playing now.

"The league now is everybody just, 'Do you' — white, Black, or indifferent."

Jason Reid spends a considerable amount of *Rise of the Black Quarterback* chronicling the struggles of the pioneers and talking to many of the living trailblazers, but he also makes the case that there has never been a better time to be a Black man who plays quarterback in the NFL. Mahomes and Wilson, who just signed a $245 million extension, have immense clout.

Deshaun Watson, despite allegations of sexual impropriety, was able to engineer a trade to the Browns and received an unprecedented, fully guaranteed $230 million contract.

Reid recalled his days covering college recruiting and how elite quarterback camps mostly had white faces. Now, he says, there are as many Black ones, with most going to power college programs.

"It's America being fair," Cunningham said. "It's young kids who are coming up and they're learning earlier because there's not the stigma any longer of because of a person's skin they can't get it done.

"I'm grateful they're not saying, 'Well, the Samoan guy can't get it done.' Come on. It doesn't matter what color you are."

Silverstein cautioned that the NFL is far from being post-race, citing the league's recent use of "race-norming" in its settlement with former players in the $1 billion concussion lawsuit. Didinger recalled a few years back when he turned on the TV to watch a playoff game and how two Black quarterbacks were starting and it was no longer considered a big thing.

"I was thinking about that in the context of why aren't there more Black head coaches?" Didinger said. "If you look at the past, the more Black players made it the better game, more Black quarterbacks

Describing how it felt to follow in the footsteps of previous Eagles quarterbacks, Jalen Hurts said, "When I got drafted to Philly, it felt like, I don't know, destiny." (Yong Kim / Staff Photographer)

made it a better game. The more really good Black head coaches and executives in the front office, it would only seem to stand to reason that the game will also improve if you improve on that level."

The Eagles were among the first to hire a Black coach when Jeffrey Lurie hired Ray Rhodes in 1995. And while it was Andy Reid who chose McNabb and drove the signing of Vick 10 years later, after he was released from prison following a dogfighting conviction, those decisions don't get made without owner approval.

Lurie said he takes "great pride" in the Eagles' standing when it comes to Black quarterbacks.

"I think we all know that Jeffrey is a very liberal guy. And I think this is consistent with his views on things," Didinger said. "But I don't think that has anything to do with decisions that are made in terms of bringing in guys to play the position.

"I think Jeff is just like the fans — he wants guys that can play and win games for him. I don't think he even thinks in those terms."

Hurts was another acquisition Lurie championed. He was chosen in the second round of the 2020 draft initially to be Carson Wentz's backup, but he has already exceeded those expectations and became the full-time starter last season.

He had his ups and downs in 2021, but ultimately guided the Eagles to the postseason. Cunningham and Vick praised Hurts, not only for his on-field production, but also for his composure and leadership, and McNabb has expressed similar thoughts in other forums. They emphasized the importance of surrounding him with talent and called for patience.

Hurts said each first reached out after he was drafted and that they now talk "a reasonable amount." They offer counsel on handling one of the most passionate — and critical — fan bases in the country.

"When they're with you, they are with you. Period," Cunningham said. "Yeah, we have armchair quarterbacks, but the best armchair quarterbacks are in Philadelphia. Not only will they critique you, but they're willing to say, 'You know what, my bad, I was wrong, I didn't give you enough time.'"

Hurts' future beyond this season is uncertain. And he has a ways to go before he can be mentioned in the same breath as Cunningham, McNabb, Vick, or any of the great African American quarterbacks. But it's easy to see how he wants to continue that legacy, in his words and his actions.

It's evident in his interactions with youth football players at the NovaCare Complex and at various camps. And it's evident when he lets his guard down, as he did momentarily at NovaCare recently, seemingly lost in thoughts, when he reminisced about watching the athletes he idolized growing up and how they inspired him.

"These guys are people who I admire as competitors and the way they play the game," said Hurts as he leaned back on a couch and stretched his arms out. "I really just want to be the best version of myself and set the right example for those to come and be someone that a young quarterback growing up in Houston or Philly or wherever can look up to and maybe model themselves after me."

Hurts wants to make HIStory. ∎

Jalen Hurts jogs onto the field before the Eagles hosted the Cowboys at Lincoln Financial Field in October 2022. (David Maialetti / Staff Photographer)

Chasing Dreams

Jalen Hurts spreads 'love and positivity' at his football camp

July 17, 2022 | By Josh Tolentino

Despite being situated several hundred feet away, each child on the grass field knew exactly who had just pulled into the adjacent parking lot shortly after 3 p.m. Saturday.

That's precisely when an all-white Jeep Wagoneer came to a complete stop. The driver's side door propped open and out popped Jalen Hurts, marking the Eagles quarterback's grand arrival for his youth football camp at Cheltenham High School.

"I'm here to spread love and positivity," Hurts said at the beginning of the event. "These kids can do anything they put their mind to. I've always been big on being in the community, trying to make a difference in the community. Doing that at Oklahoma to Alabama, back home in Houston, and now being here in Philly — trying to do the same thing. This is a really big day for me."

Throughout the three-hour camp intended for girls and boys between ages 6 and 16, Hurts, while sporting a green Phillies cap and a large gold Cuban link chain around his neck, made his way across the field. He stopped at each station and led groups through an assortment of football drills.

The most lively action of the day occurred during one-on-one route drills, in which Hurts would dial up a plan with his receiver and release the football from the pocket. Some of the passes and catches generated loud applause from nearby onlookers as camp attendees hauled in throws from Hurts.

"My son enjoys attending camps all the time, but this one is special," said Curtis Evans, whose 11-year-old son Caiden participated in the camp. Caiden is a quarterback for the Olney Eagles Tri-State Sports youth organization and a sixth grader at Franklin Town Middle School in Northeast Philadelphia.

"This time, he gets to see his favorite quarterback so he was very excited about this one," Evans said. "He loved how Jalen critiqued his throw because he's viewed as a shorter quarterback and Caiden isn't that tall. That's why he looks up to Jalen so much. Being a quarterback is his dream, and the greatest education you can get is that direct plan."

Hurts' camp was titled "Breed of 1." Inscribed on the back of each camp T-shirt were the pillars that Hurts wanted to build his camp around: confidence, perseverance, resolute, courage, and

Jalen Hurts demonstrates a passing drill to youngsters during his 2022 youth football camp at Cheltenham High School in Wyncote, Pa. (Jonathan Wilson / For the Inquirer)

swagger. He explained the thought process behind his camp's branding.

"Breed of 1 is instilling self-confidence in these kids," Hurts said. "Pushing them to be their best selves, trusting themselves, and chasing their dreams. It's a mentality. I don't want it to be football-related, it can be whatever you want it to be. The reality is there's so much going on in the world today. We have so many different people pulling everybody in different directions, but I want everybody to realize they're a Breed of 1. Everybody has something that makes them unique. I want to relay that message."

The message made it to Cheltenham High football coach Troy Gore.

"We need this in this city right now," Gore said. "We need our kids being active, having these resources to interact with a figure like Jalen Hurts. We appreciate him being a leader for our kids."

Hurts recalled attending former Texans and four-time All-Pro wide receiver Andre Johnson's youth camp as a young boy in his native Houston.

"I got the opportunity to meet him and catch passes from him," Hurts said. "That was a very memorable moment for me. I want to create that same opportunity for these kids today. Hopefully make it a day that they will remember forever."

"My time being here so far, people are so passionate about everything that goes on in this city," Hurts said. "But there's so much negativity, so much stuff that goes wrong. The opportunity I have is to show these kids, you don't have to choose the wrong way. This is a day of spreading love, positivity, and self-confidence." ∎

Jalen Hurts leads youngsters in a cheer during his "Breed of 1" youth football camp in 2022. Explaining the camp's branding, Hurts said: "Breed of 1 is instilling self-confidence in these kids. Pushing them to be their best selves, trusting themselves, and chasing their dreams. It's a mentality." (Jonathan Wilson / For the Inquirer)

Hungry for More

They taught Jalen Hurts how to make a cheesesteak.
His response 'truly changed our lives.'

February 2, 2023 | By Matt Breen

Jalen Hurts borrowed an apron last summer, stepped behind the grill at the FoodChasers Kitchen, and attempted to cook his first cheesesteak. And that's when the quarterback, who has looked flawless at times during the 2022 season while guiding the Eagles to the Super Bowl, revealed his shortcomings as a short-order cook.

"He wanted to put mozzarella on it," said Maya Johnstone, who owns the Elkins Park restaurant with her twin sister, Kala. "We said, 'No.' He's like, 'But I like mozzarella.' This is Philly. You can't."

Hurts called an audible, swapped mozzarella for Cooper sharp, and got to work. The cheesesteak also includes fried onions and mayo and has become a menu staple, aptly called the "Jalen Special."

Hurts was at the restaurant — which the sisters opened in October 2021 after retiring as principals in the Philadelphia School District — to film a Pepsi commercial, and his attempt at making a cheesesteak was an added wrinkle after he wandered into the kitchen.

When he left, Hurts pulled the twins aside and told them he would keep supporting them.

"We thought he was going to come back and buy a cheesesteak," Maya Johnstone said.

Diehard fans

Isaac Johnstone used to take his kids every summer to Eagles training camp, listening the whole way with sports-talk radio humming as they drove from Mount Airy to West Chester to watch two-a-day practices. Johnstone was a diehard until his son, Lance Johnstone, was drafted in 1996 by the Raiders.

The Eagles passed twice on Johnstone, who starred at Germantown High and at Temple before playing 11 years as a defensive end in the NFL. That was enough for his dad to pass on the Birds. Johnstone's other son, Brent, reminded his dad that 29 other teams also declined to draft his boy. It didn't matter.

When Lance Johnstone returned to Philly with Minnesota in the 2004 playoffs, the twins rooted for the Eagles and prayed that their brother did good. Their dad, who died in 2012, was still peeved but even their brother understood.

"He's like, 'I grew up an Eagles fan, I totally get it,'" Kala Johnstone said. "Daddy is just being Daddy."

Lance Johnstone retired after the 2006 season and the whole family — even their dad — rooted again for the Eagles.

Jalen Hurts' magic touch has impacted Philadelphia in countless ways — from leading the Eagles to the Super Bowl to lending his support to make local restaurant FoodChasers Kitchen a household name. (David Maialetti / Staff Photographer)

'Changed our lives'

When he left, Hurts pulled the twins aside and told them he would keep supporting them. He posted the commercial onto his Twitter account and tagged the restaurant. He mentioned FoodChasers in October 2022 when he was on Monday Night Football's ManningCast and told the NFL a month later that his Thursday Night Football interview had to be filmed at his favorite spot on Montgomery Avenue, which is about a post route from the Elkins Park regional rail train station.

The quarterback's seal of approval, the twins said, brought their small business a sizable buzz. But that wasn't it.

That Pepsi commercial netted them a $10,000 grant. He next connected the twins with Truist Bank, who donated $5,000 to the sisters' foundation that donates lunches to Philly students. Louisiana Hot Sauce, which recently released a Hurts sauce, now wants to partner with FoodChasers. Hurts even gives the sisters marketing ideas.

"He's just a good guy," Kala Johnstone said.

Lance Johnstone warned his sisters before the commercial that Hurts would probably be a jerk. He crossed paths with enough NFL superstars and figured Hurts would be just like the others. So Johnstone felt validated when a production assistant told the twins that Hurts would need a private room while shooting the commercial.

But when the assistant asked the twins' nephews to turn off their video games and leave the room for Hurts, the quarterback stepped in and told the kids to stay. Hurts sat on the couch, hung out with them, and played PlayStation while he waited until he was needed on set.

"My brother is like, 'OK. Not too bad,'" Maya Johnstone said.

When Hurts returned to shoot the Thursday Night Football interview, Lance Johnstone said Hurts was growing on him. And when Truist Bank called and told the twins that Hurts said he was letting them pick how he would give back to the community, Lance Johnstone finally conceded that this superstar was different from the ones he knew. Hurts agreed with the twins' idea to have lunch with the Roxborough High football team after freshman player Nicolas Elizalde was murdered after practice in September.

"He's like, 'OK. OK. I like him. He's my guy,'" Maya Johnstone said. "He said, 'Here's why I really like him. He's at the height of his career and he's sharing his platform. That doesn't happen often.'"

The FoodChasers Kitchen is thriving with Hurts under center. The Eagles QB, they said, has "truly changed our lives."

"Dad, you wouldn't believe what's happening," Maya Johnstone said. "This is unbelievable. It's dreams that we didn't even have for ourselves. He's putting us in rooms with people who we would never dream of meeting. We got laughed out of banks when we tried opening.

"This would never happen if he didn't always tell people, 'Call the twins. Call the twins. Call the twins.'"

Championship party

Hurts' marketing agent texted the sisters to see if the restaurant could open for Hurts and his family if the Eagles won the NFC championship. Of course, they said. They prepped the food in the morning, took the Broad Street Line to the Linc, and cheered like crazy for the Birds as they knew a win meant they were cooking for the quarterback.

"We're cheering extra hard," Kala Johnstone said.

They hustled back to Elkins Park and jumped in the kitchen. A few hours after the win, Hurts — his NFC championship hat still on his head — arrived at FoodChasers with 15 friends and family.

They stayed until after midnight as they ate a dinner that included ribeyes, chicken, sweet potatoes, a "Jalen pasta," macaroni and cheese,

Jalen Hurts makes a video call to teammate A. J. Brown as Hurts spends time with students from Philadelphia's Middle Years Alternative school in August 2022. (David Maialetti / Staff Photographer)

wings named after Hurts, and of course the Jalen Special cheesesteak.

The sisters said they were in tears. The Eagles just punched their ticket to the Super Bowl and the quarterback picked their restaurant — a Black-owned business opened less than two years ago that they dreamed about owning for years — for his celebration. They told Hurts how thankful they were. He stopped them.

"He said, I see what you're doing with kids in the community," Maya Johnstone said. "I actually admire you. All I want to leave you with is dream bigger.

Let's do something bigger now. I give something to you and you give something to someone else."

A day later, they thought about ways to meet the QB's challenge and pay it forward. Their relationship with Hurts has inspired them to keep their dream going. And it started with the mistake of putting mozzarella on a cheesesteak.

"That's the only flaw we found in Jalen and we're not even considering that a flaw," Kala Johnstone said. "He can't always have the perfect game." ∎

The Future Is Bright

Jalen Hurts seems too good to be true. The Eagles and their fans already believe he is.

April 25, 2023 | By Mike Sielski

They don't keep track of such things, but it seems a safe bet that Jalen Hurts leads the NFL in pithy expressions. Consider just the Eagles' last two games. After the team's victory over the 49ers in the NFC championship game, Hurts was asked about being benched in college. He said: "As the times change, the character doesn't." After the Eagles' loss in Super Bowl LVII, he asserted: "You either win or you learn." Even then, deep into the postseason, he was adding to his total, separating himself from the pack. The man is unstoppable.

His aphoristic relentlessness continued Monday morning at the NovaCare Complex, during his first group media availability since the announcement that he and the Eagles had agreed to a five-year contract extension worth as much as $255 million. Someone asked Hurts why he was content to sign a deal that was half a decade long and that wasn't fully guaranteed. Couldn't he and his agent, Nicole Lynn, have negotiated a shorter extension that got Hurts to free agency quicker and assured him more cash? Sure, that kind of extension probably would have chewed up more of the Eagles' salary-cap space and limited their spending power, but at least Hurts would have gotten every dollar he could have.

"Money is nice," Hurts said. "Championships are better."

We do love our press conferences in Philadelphia, and Hurts delivers the goods in that regard as well as any sports figure here in recent history. These public interactions are always part truth and part performance art for the athletes, coaches, and executives who are obliged to engage in them, and Hurts, to a degree, is no different. Those who ask him questions threaten to taint him with "rat poison." He gives cagey, mysterious answers to fend off prodding reporters. He does his best not to let anyone on the outside inside.

Through all of that parrying and riposting, though, Hurts so far has managed to win over people here, and he has done so in a way that two of his predecessors, Donovan McNabb and Carson Wentz, really never did. He has the added advantage, of course, of being as close to a real-life Rocky story as a franchise quarterback can be, but it's more than that.

McNabb could be flat-out goofy at times. He tried to make jokes and often the punchlines didn't land. He strummed that air guitar before the Eagles got destroyed in a playoff game against the Dallas Cowboys. There was a looseness in his game that

Jalen Hurts speaks during an April 2023 press conference to announce that Hurts and the Eagles had agreed to a five-year, $255 million contract extension. (Monica Herndon / Staff Photographer)

developed as the years went on, as he put on extra pounds and injuries piled up. As for Wentz, at his worst it was as if he would rather make a spectacular unsuccessful play than a safe and smart successful one, and he always struggled to accept his measure of the blame for a loss or a poor performance. Repeating the phrase "That one was on me" a few times would have gone a long way for him.

Hurts has been more disciplined and controlled than either of them, in his play on the field and in the manner he carries himself off it. Give the Eagles credit for this: As badly as they misread Wentz's character when they drafted him in 2016, Hurts has validated the core reason that they were willing to take a chance on him in the second round in 2020. They didn't know how good he would be. What they believed, and banked on, was that he would do everything he could to ensure he was as good as he could possibly be.

"When you have the talent, what [are] the odds of that person really maximizing every ounce of their talent today and in the future?" Eagles chairman Jeffrey Lurie said. "That was really an evaluation of Jalen that superseded probably a lot of general consensus at the time."

To have watched his development over the subsequent three years and to see him Monday, on that dais, was to understand why the Eagles felt confident in that evaluation. Hurts has a gravity and a sincerity to him that appeal to the hardest of the hard-core football followers here. In Philadelphia, an athlete has to show — really show — that winning means more to him or her than the spoils of stardom and celebrity. In Philadelphia, an athlete has to make it clear that he or she cares as much as the fans do. In Philadelphia, if you try, people will love you forever.

Jalen Hurts, from every available indication, tries. And he insisted Monday that his new wealth will change nothing about his approach. That the endorsement opportunities that will be available to him now and the ratcheted-up pressure to return to and win a Super Bowl will not prevent him from "keeping the main thing the main thing." That he will continue to try.

It's the highest of standards that he has set for himself, and people here will hold him to it at the same time that they adore him for it.

"I play this game because I love the game — not for any other reason," he said. "I truly love the game, and I hate to lose. In a team sport, you get a certain type of thrill and gratification from doing that with someone else, from putting that work in with someone else, from everybody committing to one common goal and trying to achieve that goal in the end. That's what made us so special, and that's what's evolved in my three years here, and that's the precedent we want to set for the future."

Quick. Someone get some smelling salts. Another half a million just hit the deck. ■

Explaining the team-friendly terms of his contract extension, Jalen Hurts explained, "Money is nice. Championships are better." (Monica Herndon / Staff Photographer)